100
GREATS

BRISTOL
FOOTBALL CLUB (RFU)

Bristol won the John Player Cup in 1983, defeating Leicester 28-22 in a magnificent match at Twickenham. The squad enjoyed lengthy and thoroughly deserved celebrations after the game and recorded a version of 'Rock on Champions'. Here club captain Mike Rafter conducts his players in a rehearsal. Behind him are, from left to right: Alan Ramsey (team secretary), Phil Cue, Alan Morley, Peter Stiff, David Palmer, John Doubleday (obscured), John Carr, Ralph Knibbs and Richard Harding (partially obscured), Peter Polledri, David Tyler (coach), Bob Reeves (assistant coach), Kevin Bogira, Mark Tomlin, Alf Troughton, Bob Hesford (partially obscured) and Nigel Pomphrey.

100 GREATS

BRISTOL
FOOTBALL CLUB (RFU)

COMPILED BY
DAVE FOX & MARK HOSKINS

TEMPUS

Cover illustration:
Club captain Dave Rollitt (right) with Mike Collins prior to Collins'
last appearance for Bristol against Liverpool in May 1971.

First published 2003

Tempus Publishing Limited
The Mill, Brimscombe Port,
Stroud, Gloucestershire, GL5 2QG

British Library Cataloguing in Publication Data.
A catalogue record for this book is available from the British Library.

ISBN 0 7524 2735 0

Typesetting and origination by Tempus Publishing Limited
Printed in Great Britain by Midway Colour Print, Wiltshire

Foreword

In my opinion, Rugby Union is quite simply the greatest team sport in the world. It caters for every shape and size, and calls for a range of abilities, from enormous power, searing pace and the most subtle of ball skills. In this, their third book on the history of the Bristol club, Dave Fox and Mark Hoskins rightly turn their attention to some of the players who have demonstrated those qualities over the last 114 years.

What a job they have taken on! The gathering in of the information about individual careers must have been a gargantuan task in itself, a true labour of love. But they have also bravely put themselves in the firing line by nominating their choices of the best players ever to play for Bristol. I have no doubt at all that you'll enjoy reading about their selections and they are bound to provoke entertaining debate, both about some of those included and others who have been left out. And what fun there is to be had from composing our own best Bristol XV of all time.

It's only when you read through a book such as this one that you get a sense of the long journey that the Bristol club has undertaken since its birth in 1888 and the huge differences in the players over the period. For the vast majority of the time, rugby union was the preserve of talented and enthusiastic local lads who fitted their sport around work and other commitments. These days the top players are professional, plying their trade around the globe. As a result it's very difficult, if not impossible, to come to a conclusion about how the players of yesteryear would fare in today's Premiership.

As the statistics show, modern players are certainly taller and heavier than their earlier counterparts. They may run faster, make more tackles and bring greater strength to the game. But who is to say what a Sam Tucker or a Len Corbett could have achieved if they had been able to concentrate 100 per cent on their rugby, benefiting from modern nutrition and training methods? And it's an intriguing thought to wonder how good today's internationals would be if they only trained once or twice a week and had to do a morning's work down at the factory before playing on a Saturday afternoon.

One thing I am sure of is that amateur or professional, ancient or modern, all the marvellous young men who have turned out for the club over the years are owed a debt of gratitude from the supporters who have had the pleasure of watching them. So whilst you enjoy reading about the very best and celebrating their achievements, spare a thought for the hundreds who don't get a mention in this book, because each and every one of them played their part in a glorious history.

Malcolm Pearce
October 2002

Introduction and Acknowledgements

Writing a book which focuses upon one hundred great players from a list of several thousand is a challenge. In truth, it is a series of challenges, particularly when decisions about inclusion and exclusion are shared between two people. Also, by including the players we have, we leave ourselves open to criticism. Why was so-and-so included? What about him? He shouldn't be there! He was rubbish! I can't understand why he isn't there. And so on. It is a personal choice.

So how did we decide on those we have included? Of course, each player must be highly talented, but we decided the primary factor was their contribution to the club. Truly great rugby players such as Haydn Tanner, Frank Bunce and Mark Robinson have played for Bristol, but they only spent a relatively short period of time showing off their talents to the Bristol supporters. Others showed greater commitment and energy, loyalty and passion for the club. It is these that we have considered the great players. Working from these criteria, we independently drew up lists of players. We agreed on 93, and discussed and negotiated the others. There are some omissions we are a little uncomfortable with. For example, we have reluctantly discarded England and Lions lock Simon Shaw, full-backs Tom Wells, Josh Lewsey and Huw Duggan, outside halves Robin Standing, Richard Sharp, Paul Burke and Arwel Thomas, scrum-half Robert Jones, hooker David Palmer, props Tony Rogers, Daryl Hickey and current player Paul Johnstone, and flanker Martin Corry to name but a few. We have added a list of additional players who have made 100 or more first-team appearances. To those players who have been excluded and their fans who believe they should be there, we extend our apologies.

We also drew a line at the end of the 2001/02 season. Would it have been a different list if done a year later? Quite possibly, with Phil Christophers, David Rees, Neil McCarthy, Ben Sturnham and Lee Best challenging with Johnstone for inclusion.

We would like to thank Gordon Lovell, secretary of Bristol Rugby Former Players, for providing contact details for many retired players, and Justin Hopwood, who provided introductions to the current players. Thanks also to Timothy Auty, Irene Base, Ian Bell, Christine Blake, Robert Davies, Huw Duggan, Kay Eastman, Tom Mahoney, Piers Morgan, John Murphy, Julie Nicholson, Phillip Payne, David Perkins, Jean Pratten, Shirley Rollitt, Ray Ruddick, Ray Shaw, Sheila Shaw, Peter Stiff, Geoff Tucker, Peter Tucker, Jen and Keith Utteridge, Peter Watts and the Watts family, Janet Wembridge, Alan Whaits, Sean Wills, James Wood, John Williams of Bristol Record Office, to Bunty for her support and, of course, to all of our families. Our thanks also go to the players for their contribution on the rugby field and their time and consideration off it.

We would also like to thank Malcolm Pearce, both for his excellent foreword to this book, and his contribution to Bristol in its troubled professional days. He is rare amongst the money-men of today's rugby: a true lover of the game.

This book would be incomplete were it not for the generosity and massive contribution of the club's statistician Neil Williams. Neil's tireless work pouring over newspapers and minute books to compile lists of statistics is very much appreciated. Unless otherwise stated, county appearances in this book are for championship or tourist games only, and club statistics are as at the end of the 2001/02 season. As we delve deeper into the history of the club and as more sources are made available to us, we inevitably increase our knowledge and discover that we have made errors in the past. Alert readers may notice minor factual discrepancies between this volume and our previous two books about the club. In such cases it should be assumed that the current information is correct. Having compiled two previous books on Bristol which told the history of the club through photographs and memorabilia it is now time to look at the contribution of the players who were part of that history. It is our hope that we have done them justice.

Dave Fox and Mark Hoskins, October 2002

Leading Bristol players not included among the 100 Greats

Phil Adams	195	Eustace Meyer	139
W.C. Allen	126	Roy Muller	108
Adrian Bain	124	Andy Munden	141
Craig Barrow	127	Barry Nelmes	154
Wally Bryant	121	John New	105
Sid Carey	176	Bob Orledge	114
Robbie Carter	220	Dave Palmer	263
Bill Claridge	105	B. Parsons	155
Michael Corbett	124	Phil Patten	156
Don Cummins	131	Bob Pearce	144
Roy Dash	160	Dave Phillips	204
Len Davies	171	John Radford	166
Geoff Davis	122	Tony Rogers	250
Huw Duggan	231	Frank Scott	106
Frank Duggan	108	John Scott	225
Harold Evans	109	Arthur Sheppard	107
Frank Feltham	176	Craig Short	130
Harold Feltham	193	Matthew Skuse	100
Jon Gabitass	123	Keith Smith	172
Denzil Golledge	116	Rod Speed	131
Steve Gorvett	196	Tom Spoors	169
Derek Griffiths	134	Barty Stinchcombe	169
Roger Grove	153	Peter Storkey	147
Billy Hale	198	Roger Swaffield	120
Jack Hazell	135	Dave Thomas	143
Daryl Hickey	143	Alf Troughton	236
Dave Hinkins	221	Alf Tucker	116
George Hogarth	105	John Watson	204
Clive Hollister	102	Jimmy Watts	130
Wayne Hone	143	Tom Webb	132
'Gaffer' Jones	199	Tom Wells	105
Edward Kibbey	194	Fred Williams	114
Paget Lambert	191	Percy Williams	146
John Lane	117	Doug Woodman	138
Mike Lawrence	103	Dave Woodward	117
Ken Lewis	135	Bill Woodward	119
Alf Lillicrap	147	Billy Wring	120
Gordon Lovell	140		
Neil Mayne	106	Up to end of 2001/02 season, numbers refer to
Eric McCall	103	official appearances for the club.

100 Bristol Greats

Garath Archer
Malcolm Baker
Stuart Barnes
Jimmy Barrington
Terry Base
Andy Blackmore
John Blake
Kevin Bogira
Kyran Bracken
Ron Bridgeman
John Broad
Alex Brown
Tom Brown
Don Burland
John Carr
Cecil Carter
Bob Challis
Bunny Chantrill
Al Charron
Paul Collings
Mike Collins
Peter Colston
Felipe Contepomi
Len Corbett
Fred Coventry
Gordon Cripps
Phil Cue
John Currie
John Doubleday
Bev Dovey
Percy Down
Andy Dun
Mike Ellery
Derek Eves

Mike Fry
George Gibbs
Jimmy Glover
George Green
Gordon Gregory
Jack Gregory
Charlie Hannaford
Richard Harding
Dick Hawkes
David Hazell
Bob Hesford
Alistair Hignell
Fred Hill
Simon Hogg
Archie Hore
Roger Hosen
Paul Hull
Wallace Jarman
Billy Johnston
Ralph Knibbs
Peter Knight
Bert Macdonald
Lloyd Mathias
Norman Moore
Alan Morley
Ronnie Morris
Charlie Murphy
Maurice Neale
Derek Neate
Tony Nicholls
Jimmy Oates
Arthur Payne
Alan Pearn
Agustin Pichot

Reg Pickles
Ken Plummer
Peter Polledri
Nigel Pomphrey
Doug Pratten
John Pullin
Reg Quick
Mike Rafter
Bill Redwood
Mark Regan
Dave Rollitt
Alan Sharp
Mervyn Shaw
Austin Sheppard
Harry Sherman
Harry Shewring
David Sorrell
Jack Spoors
Peter Stiff
Mark Tainton
Tommy Thompson
John Thorne
Frank Tucker
Sam Tucker
David Tyler
Dave Watt
Laurie Watts
Jonathan Webb
David Weeks
John White
Chris Williams
Don Woodward

The twenty who appear here in **bold** occupy two pages instead of the usual one.

Garath Archer

Born: 15 December 1974

Career: 1995-2002

Appearances: 89 games

Representative Honours: England Colts, Schools 18 Group, and U21s, Army, Durham, the North, England A, England

Tries: 11

Points: 55

Garath Archer has provided the stiff backbone to the Bristol pack during recent seasons. Never one to take a backward step, the tough, abrasive and uncompromising Archer was a crucial figure in the Bristol side that was runner-up in the Zurich Championship, and secured a place in the Heineken European Cup for the first time, at the end of the 2001/02 season.

A native of the north-east, he was named after the legendary Gareth Edwards but the curious spelling of his first name is a mystery even to him. He was inspired to play rugby by his father, Stuart, a wing in Gosforth's cup-winning sides of the 1970s. However his mentor was his grandfather, Jim Brown, a rugby enthusiast who drove his talented grandson to training and matches whenever he could. He also encouraged him to set goals and achieve them, and it was poignant that a week after Archer won his first England cap his grandfather passed away after a long illness.

As a youngster Archer found rugby an outlet for his energies. He played rugby for Westoe and Durham City before making his debut for Newcastle Gosforth as a seventeen year old. An apprentice carpenter, he had time off to play rugby but eventually this became a problem. He joined the Army and served in The Royal Signals, and his rugby career blossomed in an environment where there were less rigid demands on time. He represented the Army in the 1994/95 Inter-Services tournament.

Archer joined Bristol when stationed with the Army at Colerne. He made his club debut

against Leicester in April 1995, and was first capped for England against Scotland as a twenty-one year old in 1996.

However, rugby had become a professional sport and cash-rich Newcastle commenced a recruitment campaign which brought many leading players to Tyneside. Archer was one, and he left to return to his home town at the end of the 1995/96 season and resigned from the Army.

He remained with Newcastle for three seasons during which they won the 1997/98 Allied Dunbar Premiership title. He was a key member of that team, and he won further England caps. He later played in the World Cup and throughout the inaugural Six Nations Championship.

Archer returned to Bristol for the 1999/2000 season and formed a successful second-row partnership with Alex Brown. Prominent in the loose, in 2001/02 Archer held the pack together in the tight. Garath Archer remains a Bristol player but is preparing a future away from the game: he is managing director of Archers Marquees.

Malcolm Baker
Back row

Born: 17 September 1949

Career: 1976-88

Appearances: 234 games

Representative Honours: Gloucestershire, South West Division, England B

Tries: 52

Points: 208

Malcolm Baker, a versatile, supremely fit and often underrated back-row forward played for local club Aretians for ten years, captaining the side from 1972-75. He attended Henbury School, where Bristol player Roy Dash was a sports master, and played a lot of his early rugby in the second row. He came to the attention of the Bristol selectors after starring for the Bristol Combination XV against Bristol United. He came relatively late to senior rugby, making his Bristol first-team debut against Clifton in April 1976 in what was the final match played at Clifton's old Eastfield Road ground.

Baker was unfortunate that his Bristol career coincided with those of such back-row stars as Peter Polledri and Mike Rafter, but he nevertheless managed to play 234 first-team games, scoring 52 tries. Always a prolific try-scorer, towards the end of his regular playing days he scored 23 tries in just 20 Bristol United matches in 1983/84, as well as managing twelve for the first team. During this season the United held a ground record until the final game of the season, when Old Redcliffians won on the Memorial Ground.

Despite the abundance of back-row talent

at Bristol, Baker was able to attract the eye of the England selectors, and he toured Romania with England B in 1978, having just completed a successful season of 36 games for Bristol. Baker appeared in both tour matches, scoring a try in the 22-3 victory over Bucharest and playing in the 13-12 win against Romania B. He played for the South West against the South at Exeter in 1977 and in 1979 he was selected to play for Gloucestershire against Somerset and Cornwall. A versatile player, Baker was able to stand in at various positions for Bristol and played as both a full-back and a prop in emergencies.

In 1984/85, the season after his remarkable try-scoring feats, he was invited to captain Bristol United but he only played sixteen games of what was a particularly successful United season, as he was called up for the first team on 24 occasions, scoring 12 tries in the process. His final first-team game was on a bitterly cold night at Kelso during Bristol's centenary tour of Scotland in 1988. By this time he was on the club's committee, where he eventually served as chairman of rugby. He continued to make odd appearances for the United right up until 1993/94 and at the time of writing he still organises and plays for the Former Players XV. He has also coached at Aretians and served on the committee there.

Stuart Barnes
Outside half

Born: 22 November 1962

Career: 1983-85

Appearances: 52 games

Representative Honours: Welsh Schools, England U23, Barbarians, South West Division, England, British Lions

Tries: 16

Conversions: 99

Penalties: 69

Drop Goals: 4

Points: 481

Stuart Barnes had a brief but influential career with Bristol. The club would not have reached the 1983 and 1984 Cup finals had it not been for the contribution of this confident and ambitious player. Born in England but brought up in Newport, Barnes was a talented sportsman. He represented Gwent schools at cricket and athletics, and trained with Cardiff City. He was a precocious rugby talent, and won a record number of caps for Welsh Schools, later becoming captain.

He joined Newport and was outstanding in the 1980 Snelling Sevens. He played for Newport whilst an Oxford University student and won Blues between 1981 and 1983. Barnes was selected for the Wales squad for their 1981 game against the President's XV and remained in the squad throughout 1982, but just as a full cap seemed close Barnes, an Englishman, opted for England. He left Newport and joined Bristol in March 1983.

Barnes's arrival meant that Bristol captain Mike Rafter suddenly had the final part to the jigsaw which formed his team. Barnes only played nine games that season, but crucially these included the Cup semi-final at Coventry and the victorious final against Leicester. Possessing an extraordinary instinct for the break, Barnes was a dangerous attacker and a good distributor of the ball. His kicking

from hand was accurate, and his consistent goal kicking was an important factor in the cup success.

The following season, Barnes's kicking was even more important. Victory at Waterloo and a close semi-final win over Harlequins were attributable to Barnes and his boot. It was ironic, therefore, that his narrow penalty miss at the end of the 1984 final should rob Bristol of victory.

He played for an England XV against a President's XV in 1984 and won his first cap against Australia soon after. He toured New Zealand with England in 1985. A County Championship winner with Gloucestershire, he also played for the South West against Fiji, New Zealand, Australia and Romania in the 1980s.

However, Bristol failed to provide the ambitious Barnes with the career prospects and challenges he required. He was attracted to Bath's progressive approach where Jack Rowell was starting to make an impact and where many England friends were playing. Barnes left Bristol and joined Bath during the summer of 1985. He achieved great success with Bath, later captaining the club. He scored 18 points in the South West's victory over Australia in 1988 and was a British Lion in 1993. Stuart Barnes is now a rugby writer, and a broadcaster with Sky TV.

Jimmy Barrington
Outside Half

Born: 8 July 1908

Died: 13 September 1973

Career: 1930-37

Appearances: 151 games

Representative Honours: Somerset, Gloucestershire & Somerset XV, England

Tries: 35

Drop Goals: 13

Points: 157

Jimmy Barrington was one of the most influential players to have worn the blue and white jersey of Bristol. He was the catalyst of all Bristol attacking moves and a supreme entertainer. The local press described him as a 'dashing runner able to bamboozle defences'. He had a remarkable ability to break defences and to set up tries. He was undoubtedly one of the finest outside halves to play for Bristol during the club's history, arguably the finest of them all.

Barrington made a spectacular debut for Bristol in a rare victory over Cardiff in September 1930. He scored two tries in a 28-14 win at Cardiff Arms Park, and immediately made a name for himself. By the end of the season he had played for England and everyone knew of Jimmy Barrington.

Barrington had already played for Bristol in three unofficial games in the late 1920s, before playing for Richmond and Harlequins when studying law at London University. After qualifying he returned to the West Country and played briefly for Bath before formally joining Bristol. He also played for a combined Gloucestershire and Somerset XV

against the New South Wales Waratahs in 1928 when a Bridgwater player, and he first represented Somerset at the age of nineteen.

The rapid rise from his Bristol introduction to England international included appearances in a series of trial matches. The first of these was played at Waterloo, and Barrington orchestrated a remarkable victory for the Whites against the Colours, 45-9. This match, more than any other, showed his extraordinary running talents. He played well in the further trials and then he was selected to play for England against Wales at Twickenham in January 1931. He made his debut alongside Don Burland in an 11-11 draw.

Barrington owed much of the success of his rugby philosophy to his scrum-half Cecil Carter, with whom he played in England trials. However, Carter was never selected for England and when an unfit Barrington played outside the out-of-form Harlequins scrum-half Tinny Dean in a 6-5 defeat to Ireland four weeks later the Bristol player was dropped.

The press was in uproar. They suggested Barrington had been asked to play in a way unnatural to him. However Barrington, 'on his day the most brilliant individualist in the game at the present time', never played for England again. That *Bristol Evening World* quotation points to the reason behind Barrington's exclusion: he was too unpredictable for the selectors. There were continued calls for international recalls but they fell on deaf ears. He was a travelling reserve in 1933, but that was as close as he came.

Barrington captained Bristol in 1934/35 but damaged a knee against Bath in March 1935 and aggravated it against Blackheath a few weeks later. His knee collapsed playing tennis during the summer and he underwent an operation to remove the cartilage shortly after. He missed the entire 1935/36 campaign – for which he was elected captain – but played again the following season. He began to play more in the centre but further injury problems plagued him so he retired at the end of the 1936/37 campaign. The club's end-of-season annual report wrote that Barrington 'will go down in our history as one of the finest sportsmen who ever donned the Bristol jersey'. He did, however, go on to play one further game of rugby: for the Bristol Supporters' Team during the 1939/40 season.

After retiring from playing, Barrington took up the whistle and became a Somerset Society referee. He refereed to county standard and had the war not intervened he may well have officiated at a higher level. A multi-talented sportsman, Barrington was educated at Dr Morgan's School, Bridgwater, and Wrekin College in Shropshire where he captained the school cricket team and was vice-captain of the rugby XV. He later captained Bridgwater cricket club and played tennis to county standard. His brother was the popular Bridgwater cricketer Jack Barrington.

Barrington commanded audiences wherever he went, speaking regularly in Bridgwater on any number of subjects. After retiring from rugby he was a popular contributor to the Bristol match programme in the late 1930s, writing under the pen names 'TJM' and 'Not Now'. Originally articled with Benson & Carpenter, Queen's Square, Bristol, he subse-

quently joined his father's legal firm of Lovibond, Son & Barrington in Bridgwater. During the war he served in the RAF as a pilot officer on administrative duties. He continued refereeing and controlled many wartime games when duties allowed and refereed Bristol on several occasions immediately after the war.

Barrington was an exceptional sportsman, a gentleman, and, indeed, a real character. Len Corbett, writing about Barrington in the press, described him as: 'Rugby's untidiest player... An ancient discoloured pair of shorts and a superfluity of string in various places from the waist downwards, gave him a Heath Robinson appearance to deceive an unwary defence.' That was Jimmy Barrington: always worth looking out for.

Terry Base
Back row

Born: 18 December 1934

Died: 20 February 2000

Career: 1953-67

Appearances: 295 games

Representative Honours: Gloucestershire

Tries: 75

Points: 225

Terry Base was one of the most versatile players to play for Bristol. An academic, he was also one of the club's longest serving and fittest players. Educated at Cotham Grammar School, Base played for Bristol schools and the Public and Grammar Schools teams. He played scrum-half as a teenager and captained the National Federation of Boy's Clubs against Wales in 1951. He joined Old Cothamians and played in several positions, being big enough to play in the forwards and quick enough to play in the backs.

He joined Bristol and made his debut at Blackheath in September 1953. While he was predominantly a flanker, he regularly played in the backs during a game, when injuries robbed Bristol of a three-quarter or a half-back. Base was an immensely powerful man. A gymnast, he would frequently entertain his fellow players by walking around on his hands during training. He worked hard on his fitness and was a bundle of energy on the field. Base was also an aggressive attacker and enjoyed the physical confrontation of the tackle.

He was a key member of the side that played during the Blake era and he formed a fast and

creative back row with Len Davies and Gordon Cripps. He was a regular try-scorer for Bristol and in 1958/59 he was the club's leading try-scorer with 16. A regular Gloucestershire player, Base played in the 1959 County Championship final. After serving his apprenticeship at BAC, Base embarked on a career in aerodynamics. He studied at Bristol University before leaving Bristol in 1962 to undertake research at Brown University, Rhode Island, USA. He played rugby for Brown University, an embryonic side. They played many games around the state and travelled to play the University of Virginia. He also played in varsity rugby sevens tournaments in New York.

He returned to Britain after two years and continued engineering research at Southampton University. He rejoined Bristol and resumed his rugby career in the back row, continuing to play until leaving the club at the end of the 1966/67 season when he stepped down and joined the Trojans club in Southampton. In 1970 Base emigrated and took his family to Canada where he took up the position of Professor of Mechanical Engineering at the University of Western Ontario. He played for the St George's Club in London, Ontario, and coached the University rugby side. Terry Base, an accomplished skier, canoeist, dancer, engineer and great rugby player, remained in Canada until his untimely death in 2000.

Andy Blackmore
Lock

Born: 1 November 1965

Career: 1984-95

Appearances: 251 games

Representative Honours: England Schools, Gloucestershire, Barbarians, England B

Tries: 14

Points: 58

Andy Blackmore was Bristol's principal source of ball from the line-out for ten seasons. An athletic forward, he contributed much to Bristol's open game and was close to being capped by England. Blackmore joined Bristol from the Colts team having previously played as a junior for the Imperial club. He made a try-scoring debut for Bristol United at Nelson in September 1984 and also scored a try on his First XV debut against Clifton the following month, where his second-row opponent was Peter Brown, the father of current Bristol player Alex. His line-out expertise and athleticism were noticed immediately. He was chosen to represent Gloucestershire before he had played for the Bristol First XV.

Blackmore proved to be one of the most awkward players opponents had to deal with, seemingly possessing telescopic arms perfectly designed to win the ball. He played for the South and South West against New Zealand in 1993 and dealt admirably with renowned All Black Ian Jones. However, he suffered injuries at crucial times, most notably in the 1990/91 season when his appearances were restricted to only three games. A catalogue of shoulder injuries eventually required operations.

He added to his England Schools cap with appearances for England Under-23 and England B, but sadly Blackmore missed out on a full England cap. He toured North America with England in 1993, and played in both test matches against Canada – had it been today, caps would have been awarded. He was a full squad member but narrowly missed selection for England's tour to South Africa in 1994.

However, the game was moving towards professionalism and Simon Shaw and Garath Archer arrived at the Memorial Ground. An insurance clerk, Blackmore was happy to play for the United again but when the offer of a professional rugby contract with Coventry was placed on the table he took the road to the Midlands, along with Derek Eves and several other players. His last match for Bristol was against Leicester in January 1995 in the cup. He later returned to the city and joined Clifton. He is now player-coach with Bristol Saracens.

Blackmore, a fanatical supporter of Bristol City Football Club, is now employed by the RFU as Rugby Development Officer for Bristol and District. His job is to promote rugby within schools and clubs, helping them to organise themselves and increase the player-base. It is, perhaps, appropriate that such a physically impressive man as Andy Blackmore should have such a significant role in restoring Bristol as a rugby city.

John Blake

Outside half

Born: 30 May 1933

Died: 9 September 1982

Career: 1953-66

Appearances: 339 games

Representative Honours: Gloucestershire, Somerset, RAF, Combined Services, Western Counties

Tries: 92

Conversions: 3

Drop Goals: 32

Points: 378

John Blake was the most influential individual in the history of the Bristol club. During his four seasons of captaincy he encouraged a then-revolutionary open style of fifteen-man rugby in which attacks were launched from the most unlikely places and in which kicking was largely discouraged. Forwards ran and handled in tandem with the backs and Bristol became the premier side in the country, the style of play becoming known as 'Bristol-fashion rugby'.

Blake was educated at St Brendan's College and Bristol University and did his national service in the RAF. During this time he was stationed at Locking, played for the RAF against the Army in 1957 alongside fellow Bristol players Adrian Bain and Derek Neate, and also appeared for the Combined Services. He had made his Bristol debut in the 1953/54 season, winning his United cap, first-team cap and blazer in consecutive years from 1955.

After his time in uniform he returned to Bristol to train for his teaching certificate and was invited to captain Bristol for the 1957/58 season.

Under Bert Macdonald and Dick Hawkes, Bristol had started to play a more adventurous game and John Blake built on the foundations laid by his predecessors. He had until that time featured mainly as a centre, often partnering Somerset player Derek Griffiths, but now he moved to outside half. During his first season in charge, Bristol broke the club records for points and wins in a season. The points record was beaten again in the next two seasons and in 1959/60 the wins record was extended to 36. This season was the zenith of what has become known as 'The Blake Era', although Blake did continue as skipper for a further season, during which the appalling winter weather prevented any further record-breaking achievements. Amazingly, despite the thrilling play on offer, gate receipts dropped during these classic Bristol seasons.

John Blake proved to be an inspirational leader. He had the total trust of his teammates and accepted full responsibility for Bristol's style of play. He could remember individual games in meticulous detail and once set on a course of action would ensure that it was accomplished. He had weaknesses in his own game, notably his kicking, but he worked hard on his passing, was a speedy runner and had an eye for a gap. Training under Blake consisted of running, passing and trying out a few set moves. In matches he was a gentle, persuasive leader and an intelligent reader of a game. He nurtured a fantastic team spirit. There were times when Bristol were accused of over elaboration and tries were often conceded when moves broke down, but scoring moves were frequently launched from Bristol's own line and in all the club won 135 games out of the 184 played during Blake's captaincy, drawing 9 and losing just 40. Blake played 159 matches during these 4 seasons, frequently leading the appearances list. He remains the only Bristol player to have dropped three goals in a single game, a feat he achieved against Northampton in 1960.

Despite the obvious attractions of 'Bristol-fashion Rugby', both to the player and spectator, national selectors viewed this unorthodox approach with some suspicion and few international honours came the club's way. Blake himself never played international rugby, but he did have the honour of captaining the Western Counties team which defeated the 1957 Australian tourists at Bristol. He played in the centre along with Laurie Watts in the combined team's 9-8 victory, but was less fortunate against the 1960 South Africans, playing at half-back with Bill Redwood in the Western Counties team which lost 42-0 at Gloucester. Blake made 21 appearances for Somerset and later played 16 games for Gloucestershire. He captained both counties and also played for the Barbarians in two matches during their 1962 Easter tour, dropping a goal against Newport.

John Blake continued to play regularly for Bristol during the early 1960s. He was named as a travelling reserve for the England tour trial at Leicester in 1963 and took on the captaincy of Bristol United in 1965/66. The United lost just eight games in the season and Blake was a great inspiration to the less expe-

rienced players in his care. He made a final first-team appearance in the Easter Tuesday victory against the Metropolitan Police at the end of the season and then retired from playing. The Bristol annual report for 1965/66 included the following tribute: 'This club will always remember his play, coming at a time when the fortunes of Rugby Football required an uplift, and it was the Bristol Club that received the greatest benefit.'

John Blake taught in Bristol for many years, first at Henbury and then at his old school, St Brendan's, where he was head of history. Later he left Bristol and became head of St Wilfrid's Catholic Comprehensive in Crawley. Tragically, this much-loved and fondly remembered rugby innovator died in the prime of life, aged only forty-nine.

Kevin Bogira

Hooker

Born: 17 April 1953

Career: 1978-88

Appearances: 317

Representative Honours: Gloucestershire, South & South West

Tries: 23

Points: 92

Kevin Bogira was Bristol's regular hooker from the late 1970s to the mid-1980s. Of Polish descent, he played rugby at Lawrence Weston School and then joined the Empire Athletic Club in order to maintain his fitness. This club was associated with Broad Plain Rugby Club Juniors, and Bogira played regularly for them and for the senior side, initially as a flanker, for three seasons. He became a hooker and moved on to Avonmouth Old Boys, where he won an award for the most improved player. He also came into contact with former Bristol hooker John White and received invaluable coaching from him. He made regular appearances for the Bristol Combination side in its matches against Bristol United and was invited to play for the United in the 1977/78 season.

Bogira made his first-team debut against French side Bègles at the start of the following season. Bristol won this game, but had a poor start to the season, losing 4 out of

the first 5 matches. He was recalled to the side for the Gloucester game at Kingsholm on 23 September and this exciting 16-16 draw saw the start of his lengthy reign as Bristol's established hooker. Such was Bogira's impact and popularity that he won the Player of the Year award from the supporters at the end of the season.

Kevin Bogira made his Gloucestershire debut in 1979 and altogether made 18 county appearances. He played in the 1981 county final which Gloucestershire lost to Northumberland at a foggy Kingsholm, but was more fortunate in 1983 when he was part of the victorious championship-winning side against Yorkshire at Bristol. Steve Mills of Gloucester and Bogira regularly vied for the hooking berth in both county and representative sides, but Bogira did play for the victorious South and South-West team against Romania at Gloucester in 1985, and also played in the divisional championship.

Bristol won the cup for the first, and to date only, time in 1983 and Bogira was a member of the winning side, although he was injured during the game and replaced by David Palmer. He lost his place to Palmer in the following season, but continued to play regularly in subsequent seasons, heading the appearance list with 39 games in 1986/87. The following season was his last with Bristol, although he later served as secretary of Bristol's short-lived A XV, playing for them occasionally. He joined Bristol's committee, was secretary of Bristol United and played briefly for Clifton. Kevin Bogira also played in Bermuda for England Classicals.

Kyran Bracken
Scrum-half

Born: 22 November 1971

Career: 1992-96

Appearances: 61 games

Representative Honours: England Schools 16 Group and 18 Group, England Students, U21, and A, Barbarians, England, British Isles

Tries: 17

Points: 85

Kyran Bracken was a crucial member of the Bristol side in the 1990s. A courageous player, he made a celebrated debut for England and remains one of the country's leading scrum-halves. Born in Dublin, sport was in Bracken's blood. His mother played hockey for Ireland and although rugby was not prominent in his family, Bracken was encouraged to participate in sport. Multi-talented, he played tennis for Jersey at youth level and was an accomplished swimmer, skier and discus thrower.

Bracken was introduced to rugby with Waterloo Under-8s. Initially an outside half, he represented Waterloo, Lancashire and England schools before becoming a scrum-half and captaining the England 18 Group team. He studied law at Bristol University and UWE Law School. He won the UAU championship with Bristol University before joining Bristol whilst a student, making his First XV debut against Clifton in March 1992. It was an inauspicious start to a celebrated career – Clifton won!

An exciting player with an eye for a gap, Bracken was a consistently high performer for Bristol at a time when the side was uninspiring. He commanded great respect from his fellow players and was hugely popular with supporters. He was a great admirer of Bath scrum-half Richard Hill. Capped by England at Students and Under-21 levels, Bracken toured Canada with England in 1993 and played in the internationals, although caps were not awarded. He was promoted from the bench to the England side for the match against New Zealand a few months later when Dewi Morris dropped out with influenza. Bracken was the victim of an outrageous stamping incident early on but he battled through the pain and played a major part in England's historic 15-9 victory. He missed England's tour to South Africa in 1994 because of law exams, but was a key member of the Grand Slam winning side of 1995. He played twice for England in the 1995 World Cup and won 12 caps whilst a Bristol player. He also played for the Barbarians. Bracken's last match for Bristol was in May 1996 against West Hartlepool. Bristol's captain that day, he led the club to a 37-15 victory before leaving and joining Saracens.

He replaced the injured Rob Howley on the 1997 British Lions tour to South Africa, and has now won 41 caps for England. He was the captain of England's tour to North America in 2001. Currently the captain of his club, Kyran Bracken is one of the best scrum-halves to have played for Bristol.

Ron Bridgeman

Wing

Born: 12 December 1934

Career: 1957-65

Appearances: 85 games

Representative Honours: Somerset

Tries: 60

Points: 180

Ron Bridgeman played on the wing with distinction for Bristol for 9 seasons. A prolific try-scorer, he was very unfortunate to have been plagued with injuries and was never able to achieve his full potential. His first love was athletics. Bridgeman was Somerset County champion at 440 yards and he ran in AAA meetings at the White City.

Later a semi-professional soccer player with Weston-Super-Mare, Bridgeman, a centre forward, accompanied a friend to watch Dings Crusaders play in November 1956. The fourth XV were short of players and so he played against Old Elizabethans thirds. He had never played rugby before, but made 13 appearances for Dings before being recommended to Bristol United in February 1957. He made a fine debut against Newport United. Raw, inexperienced, but very fit and fast, he could evade tackles and score tries – he scored in every remaining United match that season.

At the end of the 1956/57 season he made his first-XV debut at Cheltenham when John Broad withdrew. He had an impressive match, in what was only his 30th game of rugby, and

as Broad retired at the end of the season it seemed certain Bridgeman would fill the gap on the wing. However, fate took a hand in the end of season sevens when he badly broke his collarbone. The injury forced him to wear shoulder pads, a rare sight at that time.

The writing was on the wall for Bridgeman. Every time he recovered from injury, he would play a few games for United, be promoted to the First XV and then get injured again. Consequently, Bridgeman didn't play as many games for Bristol as he might. On the road to recovery he played 108 games for United, scoring 124 tries in the process, a remarkable strike record.

1959 was a vintage year for Bridgeman. A regular Somerset player, he scored Bristol's winning try in a tough encounter with the successful St Luke's College side in February, and scored two magnificent tries for Bristol in a floodlit game against Newport in a spectacular and exciting match.

His final game was at Exeter in October 1964, when he suffered a full dislocation of the knee and never played again. However, he continued to be involved with the club. He looked after the players' physical fitness, assisted coaching, and was one of the club's 'sponge men' until 1978.

Ron Bridgeman was one of the finest try scorers Bristol has had. Supremely fit, he now plays tennis for Hereford & Worcestershire county veterans.

John Broad
Wing

Born: 24 May 1927

Died: 2 July 2001

Career: 1951-57

Appearances: 157 games

Representative Honours: Gloucestershire

Tries: 61

Drop Goals: 2

Points: 189

John Broad was one of the most popular Bristol players in the 1950s. A fanatical rugby enthusiast, he was a founder member of Thornbury RFC. He served as an artificer in the Royal Artillery at the end of the Second World War. An outside half, he played rugby in Palestine and North Africa on grassless grounds which were flooded after each game to make the pitch soft enough to play on the following week. This was a largely unsuccessful exercise, and going to ground became a precarious occupation to be avoided at all costs. Small, nimble and quick, Broad escaped the dreaded tackle far more than less elusive colleagues.

He joined Bristol in early 1952 when he left the army. He was initially selected at centre, but was moved to the wing where his pace and swerve could be better used. He became a regular the following season, scoring 10 tries in his 23 games for the club. Broad was one of the fittest players of his generation. He was once told by a Bristol Rovers player that Bristol rugby players trained more than professional footballers did. A perfectionist, he supplemented club training with an extensive personal training programme which he continued into later life.

He played in many of the floodlit matches staged at Ashton Gate and played for Gloucestershire on ten occasions. Principally a creator of tries rather than a try-scorer, he contributed greatly to the side in which the seeds of Bristol-fashion rugby were sown. He also helped advise the Bristol players on personal fitness, a factor which was fundamental to the successes of the late 1950s. He was elected vice captain for the 1956/57 season.

Broad stopped playing for Bristol at the end of the 1956/57 season, joined the Bristol committee and played for the Stokes Croft Old Boys club. He played once for United in 1961 to help out, and then helped found Thornbury RFC in 1963, playing for them for many years and later becoming president.

Apart from a brief period playing for Camberley, Broad continued to play rugby for Thornbury. His last game was in an international veterans tournament in Caen, France, against a Czechoslovakian side, at the tender age of 60! He was passionate about rugby, and Bristol in particular. Frequently outspoken, he left the listener in no doubt of his opinion. A personnel manager, John Broad stood for the good things in the game, its traditions and the value of its amateur ethos.

Alex Brown

Second row

Born: 17 May 1979

Career: 2000-02

Appearances: 69 games

Representative Honours: England U19, England U21, England A, England Tourists

Tries: 1

Points: 5

Alex Brown, an outstanding line-out forward, played rugby at Clifton as a five year old and attended Colston's School during the time when its rugby team was winning the *Daily Mail* Schools' Cup at Twickenham on an annual basis. Brown appeared in the winning finals of 1996 and 1997 and toured South Africa with the school in 1995. Former Bath and England player Andy Robinson was coaching at the school, and Brown was invited to join Bath's Academy. He had little opportunity for regular rugby at Bath, only featuring in a few friendlies, and was delighted to accept an offer to join Pontypool.

The move to Wales provided Brown with regular first-team rugby, and his line-out skills and all-round forward play met with huge approval at Pontypool Park. He played 40 league and 4 cup games for Pontypool between 1997 and 1999 and captained the club against Bonymaen in his penultimate game. He also played 4 games for England Under 19.

Following Pontypool's failure to win promotion at the end of 1998/99, Brown

attracted the interest of several Welsh clubs but made the decision to join newly promoted Bristol. His father, Peter, also a second-row forward, had made a dozen appearances for the club in the early 1970s before enjoying a lengthy career with Clifton. Alex Brown spent most of his first season with Bristol in the club's league-winning Under-21 side, partnering Andrew Sheridan in the second row. The first big game he started for Bristol was the 2000 cup semi-final against Wasps at the Madejski Stadium, an extraordinary occasion which saw Wasps win 44-31, with Bristol scoring 5 tries in the final quarter.

Brown established himself at Bristol in the following season, and was elected Player of the Year by the supporters. He excelled at stealing opposition line-out balls and was particularly effective during Bristol's defeat at Bath when he outplayed and outjumped the home side's future England cap Steve Borthwick. His reward was selection for England's tour party to North America at the end of the season, but an injury early in the tour prevented him from challenging for a test place.

Having played regular England Under-21 rugby, including two Sanzar tournaments, it was inevitable that further international honours should come Brown's way, and in 2001/02 he played for England A against Scotland and Ireland. It is surely only a matter of time before this superb forward gains his richly deserved full England cap.

Tom Brown
Full-back

Born: 1907

Died: 14 May 1961

Career: 1927-33

Appearances: 172 games

Representative Honours: Gloucestershire, Gloucestershire & Somerset XV, Barbarians, England

Tries: 4

Conversions: 22

Penalties: 7

Drop Goals: 2

Points: 85

Tom Brown was the victim of one of the greatest injustices of rugby history. In November 1933 Brown, who was the current England full-back, was banned *sine die* from playing rugby union because of an alleged association with rugby league. Even in the context of the times, Brown's treatment appeared harsh, and many regretted his banning.

Brown's alleged crime was to have 'discussed the advantages of rugby league'. He and three other players, including Don Burland, had taken a trip north which was paid for by a league club. Brown was in the motor trade and wanted to discuss a motor agency, while his companions looked on the venture as a day out. He had no intention of turning professional, but was caught because he accepted his expenses as a cheque, whereas the others took cash. The press reported the story and the players were summoned to a meeting of the English Rugby Union at the Grand Hotel in Bristol. Burland and the other players were reprimanded, but an example was made of Brown, and a successful rugby career came to a sudden end.

Tom Brown attended Colston's School and came to Bristol via Old Colstonians and Bristol University. He made his debut at the end of 1926/27, scoring a try in his second match, and became the regular full-back the following season. By the end of 1927/28 he was an England player, having been called up to play in his country's victory over Scotland. He played in all four internationals in 1929, although his errors contributed to opposition tries in the defeats against Ireland and Scotland. He did not play international rugby again until the Scotland game of 1932, and this time he justified selection and retained his place up to the time of his ban.

Brown, a polished full-back, was cool under pressure, had an excellent positional sense and could kick goals. Home supporters christened him 'Safety-first Brown'. He played eighteen games for Gloucestershire, including the 1932 county final, appeared for the Gloucestershire and Somerset XV against South Africa in 1931 and was a Barbarian.

Many efforts were made to obtain a pardon for Tom Brown. Ironically he never even witnessed a game of rugby league until he bought a television. Despite the best efforts of Reg Quick, Bristol's representative on the Rugby Union, Brown, who became the licensee of The White Hart at Olveston, died unforgiven. Tom Mahoney carried on the fight to clear his name and finally gained a posthumous pardon for this much-wronged gentleman in 1993.

Don Burland
Centre

Born: 22 January 1908

Died: 26 January 1976

Career: 1926-34

Appearances: 194 games

Representative Honours: Barbarians, Gloucestershire, Somerset, England

Tries: 114

Conversions: 106

Penalties: 26

Drop Goals: 6

Points: 656

Don Burland was the mainstay of the Bristol three-quarter line in the late 1920s and early 1930s. An elegant, long-striding centre, he was a hugely influential figure in the history of the club. He was born in Long Ashton, the son of W.H. Burland, a well-known Bristol sportsman who became vice-chairman of Bristol City Football Club. He was educated at Kingsholme School in Weston-super-Mare, where he excelled at all sports and captained the school soccer XI. The family moved to north Bristol and the young Burland helped found Horfield Church RFC in 1923. He played for them for a while and captained the side but as fixtures were infrequent at the end of the season he accepted an invitation to help out at the Memorial Ground and he played for Bristol 'A', as the Second XV was then called, against Chepstow in April 1925.

The following season Burland played two further 'A' games and captained a Bristol Juniors XV against the invincible Neath Schools side at the Memorial Ground.

Burland formally joined Bristol in time for the 1926/27 season. He made his First XV debut at Cardiff in mid-September, a week after he had scored a spectacular hat-trick for the A side against Swindon. By the end of his first season Burland had scored 13 tries for Bristol and had represented Gloucestershire, playing in their game against the touring New Zealand Maoris.

He was initially partnered in the centre by the great Len Corbett, and when Corbett retired at the end of the 1926/27 season the club looked to Burland to take up the mantle and lead the Bristol three-quarters. It was a hard act to follow, but Burland was more than capable of the challenge. A tall and imposing figure, he possessed deceptive pace and was able to pass accurately from either hand. These skills did not go unnoticed and he played in several England trials, the first of which was in 1928. Later the selectors recognised his raw pace and tried him out as a wing. Burland was selected to play in the centre for England against Wales in 1931. He was joined by fellow debutant Jimmy Barrington in what was to prove Sam Tucker's last international. He scored a try and conversion in the game, which was drawn 11-11. It was an impressive debut, the press observing: 'Burland can make his rivals look very small beer'. However the game was not without controversy, as his conversion was not signalled good by the touch-judges, but the referee awarded it, incurring the displeasure of the Welsh, who had never won at Twickenham.

Burland played in 8 internationals in all, scoring 23 points including all 11 in England's 11-8 victory over Ireland in 1932. He scored 3 tries for his country and was a prolific try-scorer for Bristol. In 1928/9 he scored 22, in 1931/32 he scored a try in every game played in October, top-scoring with 25 at the end of the season. He missed most of the 1933/34 season through injury but was again the leading try-scorer with 16. He was also an excellent goal kicker.

Burland was vice-captain of the club in 1929/30 and 1930/31. The following season he became captain, and led the club for two seasons. He was a regular Gloucestershire player and played in the three consecutive County Championship-winning sides from 1930 to 1932. He also played for Somerset towards the end of his career, and represented the Barbarians against Newport and District in 1933. A physical player, Burland was plagued with injuries throughout his career. Eventually he was forced to give up playing due to a severe shoulder injury. His last game for Bristol was against Aldershot Services in March 1934.

Burland refereed occasionally at Combination level in the late 1930s before teaming up with Len Corbett once more to 'advise' the Bristol backs. He later served on the Bristol committee and at one time was chairman of selectors. He also had a regular column in *The Pink 'Un* local sports newspaper.

An accomplished cricketer with Horfield Church, Knowle and Bohemians, his cricket career suffered through the same injuries which affected his rugby career. His shoulder injury was such that he was unable to bowl.

Burland worked for an oil company, and it was in that capacity that he accompanied Tom Brown, who worked in the motor trade, on their infamous visit to the north of England which resulted in Brown's exclusion from the sport. He served as a major in the

Royal Army Service Corps in the Second World War. His older brother Lionel gave great service to Bristol as team secretary of the United for many years.

During the 1960s, Don Burland became president of Cleve Rugby Club. He was licensee of The Horseshoe Inn in Downend and then ran a small gift shop in Mevagissey, where he died after a courageous battle with cancer in 1976.

John Carr
Wing

Born: 14 July 1960

Career: 1981-89

Appearances: 191 matches

Representative Honours: Gloucestershire, England Students, England U23

Tries: 127

Drop Goal: 1

Points: 511

John Carr joined Bristol whilst a student at Bristol University. Originally from Newcastle upon Tyne, he began his Bristol career as a centre but soon moved to the wing and became a potent weapon in the club's arsenal. At 6ft 3in, Carr was one of the tallest, quickest and most powerful wings to have played for Bristol. He was also one of the unluckiest, as injuries regularly interrupted his rugby career.

Educated at Hookergate Grammar School, Rowlandsgill, John Carr played junior rugby for his home town of Ryton, in Tyne and Wear, whilst still at school before making one appearance for Gosforth, curiously against Bristol in 1978. He studied mathematics at Bristol University and was first selected for Gloucestershire whilst still playing his regular rugby for the university.

He made his debut for Bristol at Newbridge in April 1981 and immediately became a fixture in the side. He scored 23 tries in his first full season and attracted the attention of the England selectors. He represented South and South West against Australia against Australia at Christmas in 1981 and then played for England Students against Fiji in 1982 but suffered an injury and was curiously ignored at senior representative level from

then on, this despite many spectacular performances for Bristol and Gloucestershire.

Carr was at his peak in the 1982/83 season. He scored a try in every round of the John Player cup, and scored two in the victory over Leicester in the final at Twickenham. He was unlucky not to have scored a hat-trick in the final. He scored 31 tries in the 31 Bristol games he played leading up to the 1983 final. He was also a member of the Gloucestershire side that won the County Championship the same season.

He played for Bristol in the sides which narrowly lost the John Player Cup finals of 1984 and 1988, and also played for the South West XV which defeated Australia at the Memorial Ground in 1988. His final game for Bristol was against Leicester at Welford Road in March 1989. He badly injured his knee, and when he subsequently ruptured cruciate ligaments in training during the summer he was forced to retire.

A devout lover of the game, he qualified as a referee and officiated at games with his knee in a brace. When he subsequently decided to try and play again after three and a half years of abstinence, he donned the jersey of Clifton. He continues to play regularly for Clifton Rats, the veterans XV, and occasionally helps out Bristol Combination clubs by playing anywhere in their back division. Away from rugby, John Carr is deputy head teacher at Filton High School.

Cecil Carter
Scrum-half

Born: c. 1900

Died: Unknown

Career: 1921-32

Appearances: 259 games

Representative Honours: Gloucestershire, Somerset & Gloucestershire XV

Tries: 28

Points: 84

Cecil Carter was one of the greatest of all Bristol scrum-halves. He was very fit, had a superb pass, and his athleticism made him a perfect link between forwards and backs. In terms of injuries, he was also one of the unluckiest players to have played for Bristol.

Carter learned his rugby at Newfoundland Road School, captained his successful school side and had schoolboy trials for England. He joined Bristol from the Imperial club and made his First XV debut away at Weston-super-Mare in September 1921. The perfectly balanced Carter was an immediate success, contributing greatly to Bristol's 31-0 victory. His pass was not excessively long but was very fast, giving his half-back partners time to co-ordinate attacking moves. He was a hugely popular player with Bristol supporters and fellow players. Small but immensely courageous, Carter was known as 'the baby of the team' due to his slight build and youthful looks. Although weighing less than ten stone, he regularly put his body on the line for Bristol, and paid the penalty for it with countless injuries.

There is little doubt that Carter would have played for England had it not been for the bizarre series of injuries suffered often at crucial times in the season. Throughout his career with Bristol he was overlooked by England, the selectors choosing instead a series of players who regularly failed on the international stage. Carter played in several trial matches, including one with Jimmy Barrington in which the Bristol half-backs beat talented opponents single-handed. On one occasion he played for England in a trial in which his fourteen team-mates were all existing or future international players. He missed the 1923, 1925 and 1926 trials through injury and although Carter was a travelling reserve for the 1924 Calcutta Cup match at Twickenham, he was never capped.

A regular player with Gloucestershire, he played for the combined Somerset and Gloucestershire side that faced South Africa in 1931. He also played in the three successive championship finals won by the county between 1930 and 1932.

He left Bristol early in the 1932/33 season but quickly rejoined and played a few games for the United before his last First XV game at Weston in December 1932. The Bristol programme of the time paid the following tribute to Cecil Carter: 'He endeared himself to the players and spectators because of his indomitable pluck, quiet and unassuming manner and loving disposition.'

Bob Challis
Full-back

Born: 9 March 1932

Died: 12 May 2000

Career: 1952-60

Appearances: 103 games

Representative Honours: Somerset, England

Tries: 2

Conversions: 70

Penalties: 49

Drop Goal: 1

Points: 296

Bob Challis was England's full-back for three of the four games which gave his country the 1957 Grand Slam. D.F. Allison of Coventry played in the opening game against Wales at Cardiff, kicking the only points in England's 3-0 victory, but injury kept him out of the next match, away to Ireland, and Challis made the most of his call-up, kicking a penalty and excelling in defence as England won 6-0. He also created something of a sensation in this game by electing to place kick penalties to touch instead of kicking out of hand. Challis won praise for his brave tackling as England went on to defeat France 9-5 at Twickenham, and in the final match, a 16-3 win against Scotland, he kicked a penalty and two touchline conversions. It had been a remarkable season for Challis, who had not even featured in England's plans until the final game of three trials played that year.

Challis only really came to prominence as a Bristol player in the season in which he gained his international honours, and he did not receive his first-team cap until the end of that season. He first played rugby at Bristol

Cathedral School and joined Bristol from the now defunct Old Cathedralians club, but although he made his debut in the 1952/53 season, a combination of national service with the RAF and the consistent play of incumbent full-back Tom Wells meant that he had to wait until 1956/57 to establish a regular first-team place. This was the year in which Dick Hawkes's Bristol side broke the club records for wins and points scored in a season, and Bob Challis played in 28 games, sharing the goalkicking with Gordon Cripps.

Rather surprisingly, that was almost the end of Bob Challis's involvement in major rugby. He was injured early in the following season and was out of the first team for a long period, and thereafter he only played occasionally, making his final appearances in 1959/60. He did not play against any major touring sides, although Somerset capped him on twenty occasions and he also played cricket for Somerset Seconds. As the years went by with no more Grand Slams, the achievement of the 1957 England team took on ever greater significance, and it was 23 years before their feat was matched. Bob Challis certainly chose a good season in which to break into big time rugby and his contribution to Bristol rugby, although relatively brief, should not be undervalued.

Bunny Chantrill
Full-back

Born: 11 February 1897

Died: 1988

Career: 1922-26

Appearances: 127 games

Representative Honours: Gloucestershire, England

Tries: 1

Conversions: 40

Penalties: 9

Drop Goals: 5

Points: 130

'Bunny' Chantrill was one of the most capable full-backs to have donned the Bristol jersey. A small but immensely powerful man, he relished the physical side of the game. Tackling was his forté, and countless attacking players were 'Chantrilled', as the local press described his powerful tackling.

Bevan Stanislaw Chantrill was educated at Bristol Grammar School, and played rugby for Clifton before the First World War. He served in the Queens Own Hussars, Gloucestershire Regiment and subsequently the Royal Flying Corps during the war.

He played for Richmond and Weston-super-Mare immediately after the war before joining Bristol and making his debut as a centre against Cardiff in January 1922. He scored a try in a rare victory at the Arms Park. After a couple of seasons during which Chantrill terrorised sundry attackers, he was selected for England. He played in all four matches in the 1924 championship in which England won the Grand Slam. He had an exceptional game against Scotland, a hugely talented side, and it was only through his courage and appetite for the tackle that England won the match.

Injury robbed Chantrill of the chance to add to his international caps the following season but the genial full-back played for Bristol and Gloucestershire. He also continued to play tennis, another sport at which he excelled. Chantrill was an outstanding kicker of the ball, both from hand and floor. He wasn't the regular place kicker for Bristol but when asked to kick goals he proved more than capable. He was also remarkably fit and used weights to build his upper-body strength, an unusual practice at the time.

In the summer of 1926 he moved to London on business. He played for Rosslyn Park before heading for South Africa to prospect for gold in 1929. His last game for Bristol was against Guys Hospital in October 1926 when Bristol made their first visit of the season to London. Chantrill played rugby for Natal before returning to Bristol in 1931. Shortly afterwards, he emigrated to South Africa and remained there until his death in 1988. He served in the South African Air Force during the Second World War.

Chantrill had strong views on the amateur ethos of rugby, and had little time for those who strove to gain financially from the game. Bunny Chantrill will forever be associated with his defence and he once said: 'I love tackling more than anything else in rugby. What a glorious feeling it is.'

Born: 27 July 1966

Career: 1998-2000

Appearances: 40 games

Representative Honours: Barbarians, Wolverines, Canada

Tries: 7

Points: 35

Al Charron played a crucial role in securing Bristol's promotion from the Second Division in 1998/99, adding essential experience, leadership and forward skills to a young side thrown together following Bristol's bankruptcy in the summer of 1998. He is arguably Canada's greatest international forward.

Charron played for Ottawa Irish and Ontario before gaining his first Canadian cap against Argentina in 1990. He played in the 1991, 1995 and 1999 World Cups, and scored the try which saw Canada defeat Wales in Cardiff in 1993. He played regularly for the Barbarians, including their victory over South Africa in 1994. He joined Bristol in the spring of 1998 after his club, Moseley, was forced to make its players redundant. He made his debut against Bedford in the Cheltenham & Gloucester Cup in March. Bristol were relegated and declared bankrupt at the end of the season, but Charron committed his future to Bristol, despite many players leaving.

The Second Division campaign began at Exeter and Charron scored a try in a crucial victory against the odds. He worked well with Mark Bennett and Jon Evans, captains during the season, and showed commendable interest, commitment and loyalty to the club, more commonly seen in a Bristolian rather than a 'foreign import'. He played in the second row and back row and his mobility and ball skills were exceptional. At the end of the 1998/99 season Bristol were promoted and Charron's contribution was recognised with the award of Player of the Year.

Charron missed the start of the following season due to the World Cup but when he rejoined, he encountered a problem. Bristol had recruited high-profile foreign players Agustín Pichot and Henry Honiball, who filled the club's overseas quota. Charron played in domestic cup and European Shield games but first-team appearances were limited. He announced he would leave at the end of the season and received a tremendous ovation from the crowd when he ran onto the pitch as a replacement against Newcastle in his last home game.

He starred in the magnificent European Shield quarter-final victory in Biarritz and played his last game for Bristol in the semi-final defeat against Pau in May 2000. Charron subsequently played in France for Pau and Dax before returning home to finish his career in Canada at the end of the 2001/02 season.

Al Charron enjoyed further success in 2002 when he captained Canada to a notable victory over Scotland, winning his record-breaking 66th cap in the process.

Paul Collings
Back row

Born: 2 January 1967

Career: 1986-92

Appearances: 179 games

Representative Honours: England Schools, South West Division

Tries: 70

Points: 280

Paul Collings was one of a succession of gifted back-row forwards in the Bristol side. Highly regarded by players and supporters, injury struck at a crucial time and his career was dramatically shortened. Sadly, his potential remained largely unfulfilled.

Although introduced to rugby by his father, Ernie, a player with Old Redcliffians, Collings was a talented soccer player, and he played for Bristol City's third team. However, at the age of sixteen he chose to follow his father into rugby. He joined Bristol Colts from Old Redcliffians and made a huge impact. In three seasons as the Colts number 8 he scored an astonishing 71 tries in 74 appearances. Bristol kept him in the Colts side where he developed into a fine forward, although he did score two tries on his Bristol United debut in 1984 at the age of seventeen, and he played twice for Old Redcliffians First XV.

An England Schools international, Collings went direct from the Colts into Bristol's First XV and made his debut at Torquay in September 1986. He played throughout the next four seasons, and was the club's top try-scorer in 1988/89 with 18, an achievement which saw him chosen as supporters' Player of the Year.

Collings was a powerful, athletic player with good acceleration and outstanding ball-handling skills. He was a regular try-scorer and formed a useful back row with Andy Dun and Wayne Hone. He played in the 1988 cup final and starred in the Bristol team that reached the final of the

Middlesex Sevens a week later.

It was predicted that Collings would have a great future. He was a bench replacement for the South & South West against Australia in 1988 and for England B against Fiji the following year, but was cruelly hit by a serious knee injury during the 1990/91 season. Rest was prescribed as treatment for the knee, and he missed half a season of rugby. His mobility and pace were restricted and when he returned to the Bristol side he was moved to blind side flanker, where scoring opportunities were less prevalent.

At the end of the 1991/92 season he headed for Australia to gain valuable experience before resuming his career in Bristol. He played for Northern Suburbs in Sydney where, in 1993, during the penultimate game of an enjoyable season, he damaged his knee so severely he was unable to play again. He was just twenty-six. Now working in IT for an orthopaedic company making replacement joints, including knees, Paul Collings remains in Australia.

Mike Collins

Wing

Born: 20 July 1942

Career: 1961-71

Appearances: 303 games

Representative Honours: Gloucestershire, Somerset, Irish Wolfhounds, Western Counties, South West

Tries: 146

Conversions: 5

Penalties: 1

Drop Goals: 1

Points: 454

Mike Collins was one of Bristol's most consistent players throughout the 1960s. Fast and powerful, he was a prolific try-scorer and is regarded as one of the finest wings never to be capped. As a youngster Collins preferred boxing, but he was attracted to rugby because his older brother played. He joined Bristol in 1961 from Bristol Saracens, where he was initially a wing forward. An outside half with Somerset Colts, the eighteen-year-old Collins was quickly promoted to the First XV after a few games for United but was selected on the wing where his speed and power were put to greater use.

Collins immediately made an impact. Playing against recognised international players such as Tony O'Reilly and John Young, an international sprinter, Collins was undaunted. He attacked players such as these with the same disregard as those of lesser fame and regularly came out on top. Tough and fearless, he possessed the ability to hit top speed almost instantaneously and had a good swerve and powerful hand-off. Collins was an aggressive tackler, highly committed and defensively sound. He was extremely popular with supporters and fellow players.

Collins was close to playing for England. Once a carded replacement on standby, he excelled himself in the South West's victory over England in the 1967 pre-Canadian tour trials but his talents went unrecognised in London. It wasn't for want of trying. He terrorised countless wings higher in the RFU's pecking order than himself, but the apparent disregard for Bristol players, other than John Pullin, for international selection meant that Collins, once recognised as 'discovery of the season', remained uncapped.

He played in several of the West Country selections against the touring teams, scoring a try against the 1963 All Blacks and contributing to the famous Western Counties victory over Australia in 1967. He also represented the Irish Wolfhounds and donned the Gloucestershire jersey on 46 occasions, at one time captaining the side.

His last game for Bristol was against Liverpool in May 1971. His team-mates kindly removed his clothes from the changing room ensuring Collins wouldn't forget his last game for the club. He joined Rosslyn Park and played for them for two seasons during which he represented Somerset.

Mike Collins, who once worked as a shipping broker, changed career and joined Courage as a management trainee. Having achieved success on the rugby field he then conquered the business world, eventually becoming divisional managing director for the brewing company.

Peter Colston
Full back

Born: 29 August 1934

Career: 1957-68

Appearances: 252 games

Representative Honours: Gloucestershire, Somerset, Western Counties

Tries: 21

Conversions: 1

Drop Goals: 2

Points: 71

Peter Colston, a full-back who captained Bristol from 1963 to 1965, later became the club's first-ever coach. Under his guidance in 1971/72 the team achieved the greatest season in its history, equalling the record of wins in a season and passing one thousand points for the first time. A pupil of St Brendan's College, Colston played for the old boys team and later taught at the school. He made his Bristol debut as a centre in 1957 and played until 1968, when he was forced to stop because of a back injury. He won his United cap in 1959/60, his first-team cap in 1960/61 and his blazer at the end of the following season in which he led Bristol's appearances with 42 games out of the 46 played, and impressed with his fine positioning, handling and tackling. In 1962/63, Bristol's 75th Anniversary season, he was vice-captain to Derek Neate before taking over as captain in 1963/64.

During his first year of captaincy, Colston made his only appearance against a major touring side when he was selected to play for Western Counties against New Zealand at the Memorial Ground. Although he was Bristol captain at the time, it was his club vice-captain, David Hazell, then captain of Somerset, who led the combined counties in an honourable 22-14 defeat. Peter Colston played in all but ten of Bristol's games during his first season of captaincy, but was not so

fortunate the following season when injury kept him out for a long period. Derek Neate took over again as captain in 1965/66 and Colston, back to full fitness, led the appearances with 42 games out of 47. This was a vintage Bristol season with only 8 defeats and Colston, who had previously made 12 appearances for Gloucestershire, played for Somerset. This was his last major season as a player. At the instigation of Dave Rollitt, Bristol's captain at the time, Peter Colston was invited to coach the team in 1969. Bristol scored a then-record 908 points during his first season of involvement and in the aforementioned 1971/72 season the team won the unofficial English and English/Welsh championships. The English title was won again two seasons later and in between Bristol reached the cup final for the first time. Colston coached England Under-23s in 1973 and the Rugby Football Union invited him to become chairman of its coaching advisory panel. He coached England from 1975 until 1979 after which he returned to Bristol as a committeeman, serving as chairman from 1980 to 1983.

Felipe Contepomi
Outside half

Born: 20 August 1977

Career: 2000-02

Appearances: 46 games

Representative Honours: Argentina U19, U21, Argentina

Tries: 19

Conversions: 82

Penalties: 122

Drop Goals: 3

Points: 634

Felipe Contepomi joined Bristol in the autumn of 2000 and made an immediate impact. Hugely popular with supporters, he was a match winner who almost single-handedly took Bristol to the Zurich Championship final in 2002. An Argentinean, he is the son of former international Carlos Contepomi, and twin brother of fellow international Manuel. Educated at Cardinal Newman School in Buenos Aires, he later studied medicine at university and has currently put on hold his medical studies at Bristol University. He will resume his medical career when rugby allows, intending to specialise in orthopaedics.

Contepomi played for the Newman club in Buenos Aires, and represented Argentina at Under-19 and Under-21 level. He starred in the 1997 SANZAR Under-21 tournament and scored 21 points in Argentina's 54-33 victory over South Africa. He made his full international debut against Chile in 1998 before touring Europe with the Pumas later that year and playing in the 1999 World Cup. He scored 21 points in Argentina's first full international victory over Wales in 2001, and was in the Argentina side which narrowly lost to New Zealand a few weeks later.

As a youngster Contepomi played rugby in the back row. At school, where rugby was the main sport, he moved into the backs. He has played international rugby at full-back and

centre, as well as outside half, and he brings a physical presence by taking and making tackles and not shirking from contact.

Despite offers from elsewhere he was encouraged by Agustín Pichot to join Bristol, and he made his debut at home in the European Shield match with Mont-de-Marsan, replacing Steven Vile. He started the next game and later scored 31 points in Bristol's 61-14 win over Parma. He tasted further success when scoring all 22 points in the Tetley's Bitter cup victory over Wasps, and scored 11 points in the club's first league win over Bath.

As an outside half, Contepomi has brought much to Bristol. He scored a league record 31 points in Bristol's home victory over Northampton in 2001. A regular try-scorer, he amassed 388 points during the 2001/02 season and set a Bristol record for league points scored in a season with 221. Six out of the highest eight individual scores in Bristol matches have been by Contepomi. In the 2001/02 end-of-season Zurich Championship, Contepomi masterminded Bristol's 27-13 victory at Leicester and scored all 32 points in defeating Northampton to secure a place in the final. Running incisively and kicking majestically, Felipe Contepomi secured European Cup qualification for Bristol for the first time.

Len Corbett

Centre

Born: 12 May 1897

Died: 26 January 1983

Career: 1919-28

Appearances: 204 matches

Representative Honours: Gloucestershire, Gloucestershire & Somerset XV, England

Tries: 98

Penalties: 2

Drop Goals: 27

Points: 408

Len Corbett was one of the greatest centre three-quarters ever to grace a rugby field. Famed for his safe hands, swerving runs, screw kicks, accurately timed passes and perhaps most of all his dummying, Corbett was a major sporting hero of the 1920s, captaining Bristol, Gloucestershire and England. First capped by England in France in 1921, when he appeared in one of his father's white vests as his family could not afford a rugby shirt, he gained 16 caps, scoring 3 tries. The first came in his third international, England's 23-5 victory over Ireland at Twickenham in 1923, and featured his trademark dummy. He caused a sensation in the Welsh game of this season by passing the ball between his legs to winger Alastair Smallwood. Smallwood promptly dropped a goal which proved to be the winning score.

Corbett played in all four games of England's Grand Slam campaign of 1924, again scoring against Ireland, and did not taste defeat in an England shirt until the game against the All Blacks in 1925, a match in which he drop-kicked a penalty. Corbett appeared in the rest of the internationals of 1925 and then missed a season before being recalled in 1927 to captain his country against Wales, thus becoming the first Bristol player to captain England. His first game as captain saw England defeat Wales 11-9 at Twickenham. Corbett scored his final international try in this game and dropped a goal from a mark. He remained captain for the rest of the season, but his final game was a disappointment, France defeating England for the first time.

Corbett first played rugby at Sefton Park School, where he was captain from 1907 to 1909. He moved on to Fairfield School, played for Bristol Schools, and had an England Schools trial, although he did not receive a full cap. After playing a few games for Cotham Park as a full-back, he joined the army in 1915 and served in France in the Army Service Corps.

On returning to Bristol he was employed by J.S. Fry & Sons Ltd and played for the works team and Bristol Saracens, before joining the interim Bristol United side which operated in 1918/19. Here he linked up with winger Reg Quick and began a partnership which was to be responsible for many Bristol tries in the ensuing years. Corbett scored 9 times for Bristol United and was a natural choice when Bristol

three of the county's championship-winning finals in the early 1920s, captaining the side in the 1922 victory over North Midlands. He was still captain when Gloucestershire lost the 1925 final to Leicestershire, and led the county team which put up a gallant show against the 1924 All Blacks, losing only 6-0. Corbett was also in the county side which defeated the Maoris 3-0 in 1926, and a year later he was in the combined Gloucestershire and Somerset side which lost 13-4 to New South Wales, dropping a goal for his team's only points in a game played in heavy snow.

Len Corbett would certainly have been an asset to the 1924 British team which toured South Africa, but although invited to tour, he had to turn down the invitation as his employers disapproved of his going. He also refused a chance to go on the Barbarians' Easter tour, allowing the Bristol committee to talk him out of going so that his presence would boost the gate at Bristol's Easter fixtures. This was a decision he was to regret in later life. He also turned down an offer to play rugby league. He retired from playing at the end of his fourth year of captaincy, although he remained active in the sport, first as a referee and latterly as a journalist for the *Sunday Times*. Corbett wrote on cricket and rugby for the paper and was a good enough cricketer to play 9 games for Gloucestershire, with a top score of 55. He was also able to follow the rugby career of his son, Michael, who played over 100 games for Bristol.

In October 1927 a banquet was held by the Bristol club to celebrate Corbett's captaincy of England. Around three hundred people attended, providing firm evidence of the regard in which Corbett was held in his native city. Once referred to as 'The D'Artagnan of centre three-quarters', Len Corbett spent his final years in the hamlet of Horner on Exmoor, and died at the age of eighty-five.

restarted in 1919/20. He scored 2 tries in Bristol's first game after the First World War, and also crossed the line in the opening game on the Memorial Ground in 1921. He was elected captain for the 1924/25 season and continued in this office until the end of 1927/28. Bristol flourished under his leadership, particularly in 1925/26, when 25 games were won and the team was undefeated until December. In 1926/27 Bristol established a new record of 31 wins in a season, although Corbett himself appeared in only 17 games.

Len Corbett had a distinguished county career for Gloucestershire. He appeared in all

Fred Coventry
Prop

Born: 1899-1900

Died: 1972

Career: 1919-31

Appearances: 335 games

Representative Honours: Gloucestershire

Tries: 19

Points: 57

Fred Coventry, who played for Bristol from 1919 to 1931, was for many years the holder of Bristol's appearance record. During the 1928/29 season he passed Jimmy Oates's pre-war record of 299 games and went on to play a grand total of 335 matches. This record was eventually beaten by Bert Macdonald, who also surpassed Coventry's 384 combined First and Second XV appearances.

Fred Coventry first played rugby at St Nicholas with St Leonard's School, a school also attended by his cousin, Sam Tucker. He captained the school XV in 1912/13, and gained an England Schools cap as a centre in a game at Leicester, scoring a try. St Nicholas won the Bristol Schools' league championship and cup under Coventry's leadership, scoring a record number of points in the process.

On leaving school, Coventry joined St Nicholas Old Boys, but enlisted in the army in August 1914, despite being only fifteen at the time. He was wounded in June 1915, and again the following year. He joined Bristol after the war and in an unusual first season played 13 first-team games, 4 in the backs and 9 in the pack. His debut was as a forward against Bristol University in November 1919, but his next 3 games were in the centre. He was on the wing against Bath in January, but was a forward in the final 8 matches of the season.

Fred Coventry usually played in the front row of the Bristol scrum, frequently with Mervyn Shaw and Sam Tucker. The three played together for the club more than 250 times. Coventry was awarded his Bristol cap in 1920/21. He gained his blazer the following

season and played in the first game on the Memorial Ground. He also appeared as an emergency winger in a game at Plymouth Albion, where a highly unusual starting line-up saw full back Bunny Chantrill in the centre and winger Tom Spoors at outside half. In 1924/25, Coventry headed Bristol's appearances with 36 starts out of 38. He played in the Gloucestershire pack in 1927/28 and 1928/29, having previously appeared as a centre in his first season.

Coventry made his final first-team appearance against St Bart's Hospital in April 1931. By then he was the highly successful captain of Bristol United, the team only losing 7 games during his 2 seasons in charge. He retired in 1931/32, but served on the committee for many years and was also a trustee of the club. In 1954 he was made a life member of Bristol. A popular and gentle man, Coventry remained close to the Tucker family and was godfather to Sam's daughter Kay.

Born: 25 September 1928

Career: 1951-62

Appearances: 291 games

Representative Honours: Gloucestershire

Tries: 26

Conversions: 334

Penalties: 188

Points: 1,310

Gordon Cripps was a goal-kicking maestro. A tall, rangy number 8, he was the club's goal kicker under John Blake, and he broke Bristol's points scoring record twice. Educated at St George Grammar School, he played rugby for the school and soccer for Downend. He joined the RAF direct from the Air Training Corps and although he didn't play much rugby beyond station competitions he later joined the Imperial club in Bristol.

Cripps was a spectator in 1946, when New Zealand full-back Bob Scott played in Bristol on the Kiwis' tour. Scott had a remarkably accurate and precise technique which Cripps attempted to emulate. When, in 1951, he saw South African prop Okey Geffin doing much the same, he was inspired. He became a goal-kicking forward to rank with the very best. He played for Bristol United in 1949/50 before making his full Bristol debut in November 1951. It was soon apparent that someone with extraordinary footballing skills had arrived at the Memorial Ground. The prolific Cripps scored 152 points in 1954/55 to break the scoring record, which he improved on with 230 in 1958/59 – a record which stood until the 1971/72 season.

Cripps revelled under Blake. He was a mobile forward given freedom to roam the field as he wished. He had a trial for England in 1954 and the following year was asked about his availability to tour with the British Lions. Sadly, he didn't tour and was never capped by England. Cripps played regularly for Gloucestershire and captained the side in the 1959 County Championship final. Towards the end of his career, he played more often for Bristol United. In 1961/62 he captained the team, which included a youthful John Pullin, and retired at the end of the season. His last match for Bristol was at Stroud in April 1962. Cripps returned to Imperial for one season before completely retiring from the game.

Cripps was an estimator at Mardons, later becoming the assistant factory manager. He then emigrated to Christchurch in New Zealand where he became a production manager. The following tribute to Gordon Cripps was published in the 1961/62 annual report: 'Gordon has been a wonderful servant to the club and his goal kicking has proved astronomical. Nowhere in the Club's records can be found such figures as he set up and those of us who had the great pleasure of watching his amazingly accurate kicking will realise that we had been watching a master.'

Phil Cue

Full back

Born: 13 September 1957

Career: 1976-86

Appearances: 274 games

Representative Honours: Gloucestershire, South & South West, England U23

Tries: 54

Conversions: 117

Penalties: 97

Drop Goals: 6

Points: 759

Phil Cue started with Bristol as an outside half but was latterly used more as a full-back. A richly talented runner and kicker, Cue was a real crowd pleaser, frequently attempting the unexpected with his jinking runs and often attacking from a defensive position. A multi-talented sportsman, he had two soccer trials with Aston Villa, played cricket for Gloucestershire Under-15s and was a member of the Gloucestershire Junior Athletics squad. Educated at Patchway High School, he captained the rugby, cricket, football and basketball teams while he was there.

Cue played rugby for Thornbury seconds while he was still at school, and was selected at both full-back and outside half for Bristol Schools. He joined Bristol Colts and established himself as Bristol's outside half during 1976/77 when Robbie Hazzard decided to take a break from the game. In the following season he scored 134 points, the highest in his career, although he was to pass 100 three more times, and appeared for England Under-23 in their match with England Students at Wilmslow. Cue, who replaced club colleague David Sorrell during the first half, kicked a conversion and a penalty but the students won 17-13. He was first selected for Gloucestershire in

1979/80 and played for the South and South West the following year.

Phil Cue, whose great-grandfather Frederick Arthur Bowdler was a Welsh international, played regularly for Bristol in the early 1980s but was unable to gain a place in the cup-winning side of 1983, although he was full-back in the losing final of 1984. He enjoyed greater glory in county finals when, after a surprise appearance at centre in the losing final of 1981, he played at full-back in the victories of 1983 (when he scored a try) and 1984. Ironically, it was his success with the county which led to his departure from Bristol. In 1985, the senior clubs decided that they could not release players to both the county and the divisional team and, as the latter was viewed as a route to international selection, most players turned their backs on county rugby. Cue however remained loyal to Gloucestershire and was unable to regain his Bristol place as a result. To the regret of many supporters, he left for Bath and actually captained Gloucestershire as a Bath player the following season. He later saw out his playing days at Clifton.

John Currie
Second Row

Born: 3 May 1932

Died: 8 December 1990

Career: 1961-68

Appearances: 89 games

Representative Honours: Gloucestershire, Somerset, Western Counties, Barbarians, England

Tries: 13

Points: 39

John Currie was an established England international when he joined Bristol in 1961. He made an important contribution to the Bristol side of the early 1960s and won his last three England caps as a Bristol player. Educated at Bristol Grammar School, where he excelled at rugby and captained the cricket XI, he then went up to Wadham College, Oxford, where he won rugby Blues for four consecutive years. A second-row forward, he made his England debut against Wales at Twickenham in 1956, partnering David Marques of Cambridge University. The pair went on to appear in 22 consecutive internationals together, featuring in England's Grand Slam team of 1957, and the hard-earned victory over Australia the following year. Currie and Marques both went on to join Harlequins, but work with W.D. and H.O. Wills brought Currie back to Bristol, the city of his birth.

One of John Currie's early Bristol appearances was in an unofficial floodlit game against Cardiff, played at Cardiff City's Ninian Park ground. Bristol, who won 20-3, produced some stunning rugby, despite being reduced to 13 players at one stage, and Currie went on to enjoy a successful season, winning his first XV cap and scoring 8 tries. He played his final 3 games for England in 1962, a disap-

pointing scoreless draw with Wales at Twickenham, a comfortable 16-0 victory over Ireland and a 13-0 defeat in France.

Despite an early allegiance to Gloucestershire, John Currie played the bulk of his county rugby for Somerset, winning 32 caps, and captaining the county on many occasions between 1960 and 1963. He also played one cricket match for Somerset, scoring 4 and 13 against Leicestershire in 1953. His last major season for Bristol was 1963/64, when he played 35 games and appeared for the Western Counties team which lost 22-14 to the All Blacks on the Memorial Ground. He later played for Northern.

In addition to his skill as a line-out forward, Currie was also a reliable goalkicker, good enough to kick for England, but his only recorded kicks for Bristol are in United games. Nicknamed 'Muscles', he had a reputation for being completely impervious to provocation from opposition players. He also once famously explained that he only jumped at the line-out in England trials when the selectors in the West Stand could see his number! An England selector himself from 1986 to 1988, Currie was chairman of Harlequins for eight years, represented the Barbarians, and captained Northumberland. He was present at Bristol's centenary dinner in 1988, but died, aged fifty-eight, just over two years later.

John Doubleday
Prop

Born: 22 January 1956

Career: 1976-93

Appearances: 314 games

Representative Honours: Barbarians, Gloucestershire, England Schools, U23, Students England XV

Tries: 4

Points: 16

John Doubleday was one of the most talented prop forwards ever to play for Bristol. Had it not been for the cruel hand of fate, he would have been a seasoned international forward. Doubleday joined Bristol during the 1976/77 season while studying at the Royal Agricultural College, Cirencester. Having previously played for Newport Youth and French side Stade Bordelais, he had an impressive rugby CV which included England Schools honours at several levels.

As a Bristol player he formed a robust front row with Kevin Bogira and Austin Sheppard, which played together as a unit for many seasons. An immensely strong farmer, Doubleday was equally at home on either side of the scrum and possessed expert technical abilities and the desire to run with the ball in the loose.

He was unusual in that he was promoted direct from England Schools 19 Group to England Under-23. He possessed dual qualification – born in Usk of a Welsh father and English mother but brought up in England. At one time he was selected for the Wales B squad but opted to pursue an England career. Doubleday was a final trialist, squad member and bench replacement for England during the 1979 Five Nations Championship. At the end of that season he accompanied the full England side on tour to the Far East, playing in the test matches which at that time didn't qualify for full international honours.

He severely damaged his hamstring against Swansea upon his return and missed most of the following season. This undoubtedly cost him an England cap. Out of favour with the selectors in subsequent seasons, he was not considered again, but remains the most-capped forward at England Under-23 level. However he did play for a World XV against Argentina in 1980, represented the Barbarians and was a regular player for Gloucestershire.

Business and family commitments curtailed Doubleday's Bristol appearances in 1985/86 and had it not been for the encouragement of Andy Dun he would have retired. He returned to playing and continued until an Achilles injury effectively ended his career during the 1989/90 season. He helped with coaching after that and played one match for Bristol United in 1991/92. He finally hung up his boots after one last game for the First XV, a victory at Bridgend in April 1993.

John Doubleday was a crucial member of the Bristol side during the 1980s. Thoroughly reliable, he played in the three cup finals and was the cornerstone of the pack during one of the club's most successful periods.

Bev Dovey
Prop

Born: 24 October 1938

Career: 1965-70

Appearances: 184 games

Representative Honours: Gloucestershire, Somerset, Yorkshire, Hertfordshire, English Universities, Barbarians, Western Counties, South of England, England

Tries: 7

Points: 21

Bev Dovey played with distinction in the Bristol front row in the late 1960s. A versatile prop, he was an England international and played for four different county sides.

Educated at Lydney Grammar School, Dovey was an England schoolboy international, and played for Lydney whilst still at school. He studied at Leeds University and Cambridge, where he won a Blue in 1960. Whilst at Leeds he represented Yorkshire and English Universities, and also played for Roundhay.

A biology teacher at Merchant Taylor's School, Dovey played for Rosslyn Park. He captained Rosslyn Park for the 1963/64 season but maintained his association with the West Country – he represented Gloucestershire and played for Western Counties against South Africa in 1960 and New Zealand in 1963.

Dovey was selected to play for England in 1963 and made his debut alongside John Thorne against Wales. He won his second and final cap against Ireland a few weeks later.

He left Rosslyn Park at the end of the 1964/65 season to take up an appointment at Withywood School, and joined Bristol. He

made his Bristol debut at Stroud in September 1965 and played 41 games in his first season. Dovey was a very capable footballer. He was an excellent ball handler ideally suited to the open style of rugby Bristol adopted. Initially a loose-head prop, he moved to tight head when scrummaging became more technical. He was tall for a prop and found he was better suited to the tight head position. It was a conscious decision made in the knowledge that there was more competition for international places on that side of the scrum.

Nevertheless, he played his best rugby wearing a Bristol shirt, and continued to feature in England trials without the reward of further honours. He was Bristol vice-captain for the 1967/68 season. Dovey moved schools and taught at Millfield. He found the travelling problematic and with family and work commitments he considered retiring at the end of the 1969/70 season. However, he had a change of heart and joined Bridgwater. He represented, and captained, Somerset whilst at Bridgwater before returning to Leeds and resuming his Roundhay and Yorkshire careers. He later rejoined the staff at Millfield.

He enjoyed playing in front of big crowds in important matches. He represented the Barbarians and captained Western Counties to victory over Australia in 1967. He also captained South of England against New Zealand later that year and played for Western Counties against South Africa in 1969. Bev Dovey relished the challenge of big matches.

Percy Down
Lock

Born: 14 October 1883

Died: 22 July 1954

Career: 1905-10

Appearances: 117 games

Representative Honours: Somerset, England, Anglo-Welsh

Tries: 12

Points: 36

Percy Down was a commanding figure in the Bristol pack in the first decade of the twentieth century. He contributed greatly to play around the pitch, and in later life became an influential administrator of the club.

Down joined Bristol at the beginning of the 1904/05 season from the Redland club, and after playing for the Second XV he made his full debut against Pontypridd in December 1905. He rapidly established himself in the team and developed a reputation as a tough player. He was a powerful scrummager and soon earned selection for Somerset.

Down was chosen to tour New Zealand and Australia with the 1908 Anglo-Welsh team. He had to give up his job to go but played in all 3 test matches, which were against New Zealand. Leaving New Zealand, Down fell overboard into Auckland harbour whilst attempting to shake hands with a friend on the quayside. British full-back Edward Jackett and All Black 'Bolla' Francis, whom Down had encountered in the internationals, dived in to rescue him. Weighed down by heavy clothing, Down struggled to keep afloat but a rope was tied around him and attached to the ship until a launch arrived to take him and his rescuers to dry land. Fortunately Down was unharmed by the experience.

Down played once for England, against Australia in 1909. England players were given a rose and had to provide the jersey themselves, but Down, a fruit farmer, was unable to afford a white rugby jersey. Consequently he played in his PT vest, with the rose sewn

neatly over his heart. Although England lost 9-3, Down played with distinction but he was never capped again. Four days later Down, then Bristol's club captain, led a combined Bristol and Clifton XV against the Australians at the County Ground. The tourists won 11-3 in one of the finest games of the tour.

His last game for Bristol was against Devon Albion in January 1910. Following his retirement he continued farming in Failand. After the Second World War he was elected Bristol's vice-chairman for the 1945/46 season, but he took over the running of the club when chairman W.J. Houlden died in office. He served as chairman until 1953/54 but died suddenly during the close season, shortly after being awarded life membership. A memorial fund was established in his name which provided for repairs and developments to the hall under the stand.

Down's son-in-law, Denzil Golledge, was Bristol captain for the 1950/51 season.

Andy Dun ────────────────────────────────

Back row

Born: 26 November 1960

Career: 1980-91

Appearances: 170 games

Representative Honours: England Schools, England Students, Middlesex, London Division, South & South West, England U23, England

Tries: 39

Points: 156

Andy Dun, a back-row forward, captained Bristol for two seasons from 1988. A pupil of Bristol Grammar School, where he captained the First XV and was head boy, he was a member of the successful England Schools 19 Group tour to Australia and New Zealand in 1979, appearing in all three 'tests'. He made his Bristol debut against Metropolitan Police in 1980 and was named *Evening Post* 'man of the match' for his contribution to a 23-3 victory.

Dun played six games during his first season, but then moved to London to train at St Bartholemew's Hospital and, after playing once for London Scottish, joined Wasps. He played for England Students, captaining them on their tour to Japan in 1983, and skippered the England Under-23 tour to Italy a year earlier. He went to Romania with England Under-23 in 1983, played for Middlesex, and appeared for London Division against the 1981 Australians.

Dun was vice-captain of Wasps in 1983/84, but led the side for much of the season due to skipper Nigel Melville's injury. During this season he received his only England cap, playing on the flank against Wales at Twickenham, a game which England lost

24-15. He was appointed captain of Wasps in 1984, but injury prevented him from playing at all during the season.

Dun returned to Bristol in 1985, played 29 matches, scoring 13 tries, and appeared for the South and South West. He played regularly during the next two seasons and was in the team which lost the 1988 cup final against Harlequins. Dun was the obvious choice to succeed Nigel Pomphrey as skipper, and became the first captain of the club's second century, winning his club blazer in 1989. His first season in charge saw Bristol defeat Cardiff twice in a season for the first time since 1930/31. This was also the season when Bristol were involved in a remarkable cup quarter-final at Bath, played on a near-waterlogged pitch. Dun and Bath captain Stuart Barnes, had disagreed as to whether the game should go ahead and they left it to the referee to make the final decision. Bristol led for much of the game, but conceded a late try and lost 14-12.

Andy Dun's second year of captaincy saw Bristol lead the Courage League early on, then fail to win another league game until the final match of a disappointing season. Dun played 11 games for Bristol during 1990/91, but then retired from the game.

Mike Ellery
Wing

Born: 24 August 1933

Career: 1954-66

Appearances: 347 games

Representative Honours: Gloucestershire, Western Counties

Tries: 251

Points: 753

Mike Ellery was one of the finest wings ever to have graced a Bristol side. He was a devastating runner who provided the icing on the rich cake that was the Blake era – the scoring of tries. His 251 tries for Bristol stood as the career record until Alan Morley overhauled it many years later. But even the great Morley couldn't exceed the record of 44 tries Ellery scored in the 1961/62 season.

Ellery was educated at Colston's School where he was not regarded as a rugby player. However, outside school he rose rapidly through local rugby to play for Bristol. An outside half in the same Cleve Juniors side as John Thorne, he subsequently played on the wing for Cleve in a handful of games before being invited to the Memorial Ground. After one game in the United he made his First XV debut against Swansea in September 1954.

He possessed blinding acceleration, a gift which took him past virtually all his opponents. Blake's open rugby philosophy allowed him turn up anywhere on the field and Ellery became a devastating weapon in Bristol's arsenal. Blake gave him *carte blanche* to do what he thought best. Although predominantly a right wing, he scored as many tries on the left.

Ellery played little rugby when on National Service in the Royal Signal Corps. Originally involved in the sale of natural oils, during his rugby career he was a raw materials buyer for an animal feed company and later became a grain broker. He was an elegant, confident player and was able to swerve at top speed. He approached rugby in a professional manner. He sprinted for Bristol Athletic Club, and ran for Gloucestershire, specialising in the 220 yards. He used athletics principally as a means of training for rugby and enhancing his rugby skills.

These skills were never fully recognised at national level. He had a trial for England in 1958 and represented Western Counties against South Africa in 1960, but international appearances never came. It is not clear why his skills were not deemed desirable by the national selectors. It is probable that the style of rugby Bristol were playing didn't fit in with the narrow, unimaginative approach England adopted at the time.

In the late 1950s and early 1960s Ellery was in imperious form. John Blake and Bert Macdonald had led a rethink on how rugby should be played and fifteen-man rugby was on the menu. Blake gave that added dimension to rugby. His attention to detail brought out the best in all his players. One of the many moves in the club's repertoire involved Blake, renowned for not being a kicker, kicking behind the defence and Ellery

Mike Ellery shows his strength by handing off an opponent at the Memorial Ground.

collecting the ball at top speed, frequently before it had bounced, and scoring.

A player with a remarkable anecdotal history, Ellery scored a try for Bristol in a televised floodlit match against Cardiff in November 1961. With live coverage of club matches in its infancy, Cliff Morgan, of the BBC, was desperate to ensure that it went well and that when they were broadcasting to the nation something exceptional should occur. A prize of £5 was offered if a try could be scored when 'on air'. Man of the moment, Mike Ellery scored on cue. Bristol won 20-3, his £5 was added to the beer kitty and a good night was had by all.

The 1961/62 season was one to remember for Ellery. He scored a remarkable 44 tries in 38 games, a record which shattered the previous club best of 33 set by Reg Quick in 1920/21. Quick's record was broken against United Services Portsmouth in March 1962. However, just as the public were speculating what he would do next, Ellery broke his ankle

in the club trials before the next season and missed all but 9 first-team games that season.

He played his last game for Bristol against Coventry in April 1966 and then stepped down to play for Cleve, whilst also serving briefly as a Committeeman with Bristol, playing once for United the following season when injuries prevailed. It is remarkable, but perhaps not surprising, that after playing for Bristol for 12 seasons he continued to play for Cleve until he was 49.

When Alan Morley retired in 1986 he held the world record for tries scored in first-class rugby. It was a record he took from Llanelli wing Andy Hill, who played for the Welsh club in the late sixties and seventies. But who held the record before Hill? The answer is not known but it is quite likely that with 251 tries for Bristol plus countless others scored elsewhere, Mike Ellery, a player who scored 6 tries for Bristol on 2 occasions, and a hat trick an amazing 21 times, may well once have been the world record try-scorer.

Derek Eves
Flanker

Born: 7 January 1967

Career: 1986-95

Appearances: 278 games

Representative Honours: Barbarians, South West, Midlands, England Colts, Emerging England, England A

Tries: 88

Points: 383

Derek Eves had a celebrated rugby career in which his principal qualities were leadership and pace. Originally from Avonmouth Old Boys, he was a Bristol Colt from 1982 to 1985 during which time he scored 36 tries in his 49 games. He captained them and played occasionally for Bristol United. He also played for England Colts.

He was first selected for the Bristol team against Morley in February 1986. There was considerable competition for back-row places and so Eves spent much of his first season in the United. However, he made a name for himself during 1986/87 when he scored 4 tries against Camborne.

Eves was a player who led by example. Not the tallest of flank forwards, what he lacked in stature he made up with enthusiasm, commitment and ability. A magnificent support player, he was rarely more than a few feet away from the ball and could forage on the ground better than most. He was appointed Bristol captain for the 1990/91 season and remained in charge for five seasons. Eves held the side together when they struggled to cope with league rugby and only Wallace Jarman captained the club for a similar period of time.

Eves was a remarkable try-scorer. He was the club's leading try-scorer in 1991/92 and his career total of 88 as a forward has only been beaten by Nigel Pomphrey and Dave Rollitt. A fixture in the South West side, he played regularly for Emerging England, and captained them to a 34-6 victory over Canada in 1994. He also captained the England team that played in the 1995 Hong Kong Sevens. He represented England A and was a regular player for the Barbarians, touring Zimbabwe with them in 1994. Unfortunately, Eves was in direct competition with Neil Back for the England open-side position, although bigger forwards were more popular in that position at the time. Despite arguments for his inclusion, Eves was never selected for the national side.

As rugby headed towards professionalism Eves left Bristol and joined Coventry as player-coach. He played in 53 league games for them between 1995 and 1998 and captained the Midlands against Argentina in 1996. He returned to Bristol when they were in Division Two and had an important role in motivating the team towards promotion at the end of the season. His last game for Bristol was at the end of the 1998/99 season against Cornwall at Twickenham.

Derek Eves later became director of rugby at Coventry and he now fulfils a similar role with Doncaster Rugby Club.

Mike Fry

Prop

Born: 5 October 1943

Career: 1968-81

Appearances: 435 games

Representative Honours: Somerset, South &
South West

Tries: 14

Conversions: 1

Points: 58

Mike Fry, arguably the greatest prop forward
in the history of the club, was Bristol's captain
for two seasons. A strong, abrasive loose head,
he was ignored by representative selectors for
most of his playing career, but was greatly
respected by his team-mates and by opposition front rows, particularly in Wales.

Fry played rugby as a flanker and soccer at
Bedminster Down School, but played little
rugby for the next few years, partly because of a
motorcycle accident. He eventually joined
Cotham Park and was called into the Bristol
United side on five occasions in 1967/68. At
that time Bristol's policy was that prop forwards
should be big men and Fry, who was comparatively short, was used as a hooker in some of his
early games. The general feeling was that he
would not make the grade on account of his
size, but he played twice for the first team the
following season and received his United cap at
the end of 1969/70. During this period he
counted goalkicking amongst his skills and
often acted as the United's kicker.

Mike Fry was the United captain in
1970/71, although by this time he was
cementing his place in the first team. He
made 30 first-team appearances in 1971/72,

was awarded his cap, and played regularly from
then on. He upped his appearances to 45 in the
following season, winning his club blazer and
performing heroics in Bristol's cup-final defeat
against Coventry. Hooker John Pullin was
injured in the first minute of the game and Fry
managed three strikes against the head as stand-
in hooker in a seven-man pack. He made his
Somerset debut in this year.

Fry, whose appearance earned him the
nickname 'The Greek', became Bristol's vice-
captain in 1974/75, playing in more games than
any other forward, and he led the club's appearances with 42 games in 1976/77. He was
appointed Bristol captain in 1978/79 and led the
side for two very successful seasons. The first of
these saw Bristol struggling in mid-season before
embarking on a superb run of seventeen consecutive victories up to the season's end. Only 11
games were lost and over 1,000 points scored in
1979/80 and Fry achieved the remarkable feat of
appearing in all 95 games during his captaincy,
reaching 400 career appearances in the final
match. He eventually extended his consecutive
run to 102 games.

In 1979 he received a long overdue call-up
to the South and South West side to play New
Zealand at Exeter. Fry, who was not an
original selection for the game, was given the
job of pack leader and acquitted himself well,
although his team lost 16-0. Afterwards he
claimed that the game was no harder than
many he had played in Wales. Fry always
relished Welsh encounters and learned a lot
in his United days from fixtures with
Monmouthshire valley sides.

The only other regular representative rugby that Mike Fry played was for Somerset, for whom he appeared on 21 occasions. He decided to give county rugby a miss during his seasons as Bristol captain, but was delighted to be recalled in 1980 to lead Somerset against Devon at Bridgwater. Unfortunately, various incidents during Somerset's 18-9 defeat led to his being banned from the county team for the rest of the season. Fry certainly stood no nonsense on a rugby field, but despite his reputation he was only sent off once. This was during an ill-tempered cup match at London Irish in 1976 when Fry was singled out in a poorly controlled game where much skulduggery went unnoticed and unpunished.

The 1980/81 season was Fry's last as a Bristol player as he chose to bow out on his own terms rather than hang on for one season too many. He played 35 matches during his final year, making his final home appearance on Easter Monday in a 63-9 win against Abertillery. His fellow players did their best to provide him with a try-scoring farewell, but it was not to be and he also failed with the conversion of the game's final try. His last match was at Coventry the following Saturday, and although Bristol lost 14-4, it

was a memorable day for Fry as a presentation was made to him by the Bristol Supporters' Club before the game. He went on Bristol's American tour and then left the club. Having already coached Old Redcliffians whilst with Bristol, he joined the club as player-coach and later became captain.

Under Fry's guidance, Old Reds reached the Bristol Combination and Somerset Cup finals in 1982, losing on both occasions to Keynsham. The club won the Combination Cup in 1983 and the Somerset Cup final was reached again. Although Fry's team were well beaten by Bath, they qualified for the next season's John Player Cup and Jack Rowell, Bath's coach, was so impressed with Fry that he invited him to help out at the club, an offer he declined. In the John Player Cup Reds defeated Devon and Cornwall Police and Worthing to set up a third-round clash with senior side London Scottish. Under Fry's inspirational leadership Old Redcliffians gave their visitors a real fright before losing 24-15. Reds finally won the Somerset Cup at the end of the 1983/84 season, beating Keynsham 22-9. As a fitting finale to Fry's playing career the Somerset and Combination Cups were won again in 1985.

George Gibbs

Prop

Born: 31 March 1920

Died: 26 February 2001

Career: 1939-54

Appearances: 123 games

Representative Honours: England, Barbarians, Gloucestershire, Northumberland

Tries: 7

Points: 21

George Gibbs was one of the most influential Bristol players in the immediate post-war era. A prop forward, he led from the front and was heavily involved in rebuilding the club after the war, captaining Bristol for three seasons. Bristol rugby was in Gibbs' blood. His grandfather was W.E. Lambert, a founder member, and as a boy he watched Bristol play regularly even though his father played for Clifton.

He was educated at Clifton College, captained the school XV and organised their fixtures. Bristol United had a regular fixture against the College and after one match between the sides he was invited to join Bristol when he finished school. This he did. He made his United debut in December 1938 against Yeovil, scored a try, and played in every remaining United game that season. At the end of the season he made his First XV debut against Nuneaton.

Sadly for Gibbs, the war intervened just as his rugby career was taking off. Initially in the Territorial Army, he joined the 44th Battalion Royal Tank Regiment, then served in the Indian Armoured Corps as a Tank Commander. He played very little rugby during the war, but did make occasional appearances for the Bristol supporters' team.

He rejoined Bristol for the 1946/47 season, during which he played for England against France, and enjoyed an Easter tour with the Barbarians. He was joined in the Bristol side by his younger brother Nigel, a full-back. He became Bristol captain the following season, a position he fulfilled with great energy and dedication. He led the team on a memorable tour to Nantes and Cognac in November 1947 and famously delivered a post-match speech in French which no-one understood but himself! Gibbs also played for England against Ireland in 1948. This was to be his last international.

Gibbs worked for Imperial Tobacco and moved to Newcastle in 1950, becoming factory manager a few years later. He joined Northern and played for them for several seasons, later becoming their fixture secretary. He also encouraged John Currie to join Northern, in 1965. He continued to make occasional appearances for Bristol when visiting the city. His last game was in 1953/54, against Cardiff. He played for Gloucestershire on 17 occasions and captained them. He later captained Northumberland.

George Gibbs returned to Bristol later in life and became a governor at Clifton College. The 1947/48 annual report summarised his qualities: 'he had unusual gifts of leadership and an instinctive antipathy to anything slack or unsportsmanlike.'

50

Jim Glover
Centre

Born: 29 September 1936

Career: 1961-68

Appearances: 199

Representative Honours: Cornwall, Dorset &
Wiltshire, Barbarians, RAF, Western Clubs,
South West Counties

Tries: 44

Conversions: 5

Penalties: 1

Drop Goals: 4

Points: 157

Jim Glover held together the Bristol defence during the 1960s. A modest man, he played rugby for fun, enjoyed himself immensely, and felt privileged to have played for Bristol.

Glover was educated at Penzance Grammar School, where he played soccer. He began playing rugby when he was fifteen and in his last years at school he played soccer for Penzance FC and rugby for Penzance & Newlyn. He was also a highly proficient tennis player and competed at junior Wimbledon.

He played rugby for the RAF in Cyprus when on National Service, and represented a Middle East Air Force XV. He then read English at Oxford University and played in the 1959 and 1960 Varsity matches, captaining the side in the latter game, and against South Africa in 1960. In 1961 he took up an appointment at Clifton College without expecting to play any rugby. However, he was invited to join Bristol and made his debut against London Irish in October.

Initially a wing, Glover was moved to the centre, where he played most of his rugby for Bristol. There was considerable competition for places but his defensive play was such that he soon became a fixture in the side. He worked hard on his defence and frequently made several tackles defending one attacking move. He also had the pace and footballing skills to launch counter-attacks or kick accurately to touch.

He was a member of the Bristol team that won the club's 75th Anniversary seven-a-side tournament in 1963. He was vice-captain for the 1965/66 season and was an occasional place kicker for the club.

Glover played for Cornwall on 41 occasions between 1958 and 1967, at one stage captaining the county. He also toured South Wales with the Barbarians in 1968 and played for Western Clubs against Canada in 1962 and South West Counties against New Zealand the following year.

He left Bristol at the end of the 1967/68 season when he took up an appointment at a school in Swindon. He joined Swindon RFC and played for them for four seasons, and also represented Dorset & Wiltshire in the County Championship.

Glover later worked in Malta and played there for ex-pats sides before returning to Cornwall and resuming his career with Penzance, continuing to play for the Pirates into his early forties. He enjoyed the camaraderie offered by rugby and after retiring from the game recognised how important rugby is to many people. Still fit and active, Jim Glover now plays veterans tennis for Cornwall.

George Green

Wing

Born: 4 July 1921

Career: 1945-50

Appearances: 118 games

Representative Honours: Gloucestershire, Gloucestershire & Somerset XV, British Cameroons, British Army of the Rhine

Tries: 53

Drop Goals: 2

Points: 165

George Green first became interested in rugby at the age of nine when Monty Hamblin, his history master at Whitehall School, invited Tom Brown, the Bristol and England fullback, to talk about the game. At the age of eleven he moved to St George School where he came under the influence of Mr Morton, the maths master, who was responsible for a vast improvement in the standard of rugby there. He made his Bristol debut as a last-minute call-up in Bristol's first match after the Second World War, having previously played a few games for the wartime Bristol Supporters team. Green scored a hat-trick of tries in the 21-3 victory over Stroud and finished the season as leading try-scorer with 9 from 16 games. Chiefly a winger, although capable of playing at fly-half, he led Bristol's appearances with 32 in 1946/47, winning his club cap. He was once again leading try-scorer, this time with 21, and he was appointed vice-captain for the 1947/48 season. He led the side on its unbeaten tour of Devon and Cornwall in the absence of skipper George Gibbs. In the October of this season he arrived late for the home game with Bath but scored a try with his first touch of the ball just after he joined the fray.

Green, whose childhood inspiration Tom Brown became a close friend, was capped 12 times by Gloucestershire, played for Gloucestershire and Somerset against the 1947 Australians, and was in the Gloucestershire side which lost the 1947 County final to Lancashire after a replay. During the Second World War he served in the Royal Navy as first lieutenant of a landing craft flotilla. His flotilla took American troops to Omaha Beach on D-Day. All first lieutenants are known as 'Jimmy the One' and he retained the nickname 'Jimmy'. In his own words: 'I left Bristol in 1940 as George and came back as Jimmy.'

Green read history at Bristol University, then moved to Cornwall in 1950. There he played for Redruth, captaining the reserves to an unbeaten season in 1953/54. One of his team-mates was England international Keith Scott and the two played cricket together for Cornwall.

Joining the Army in 1954, Green played at fly-half for the British Army of the Rhine and at the age of forty achieved the unusual distinction of playing for British Cameroon against French Cameroon, receiving a special tie to mark the occasion. He now lives in Axminster and has recently appeared in television programmes about the Normandy landings.

Gordon Gregory
Hooker

Born: 8 December 1908

Died: 4 December 1963

Career: 1931-34

Appearances: 56 matches

Representative Honours: Somerset, Gloucestershire and Somerset XV, Barbarians, England

Tries: 3

Conversions: 14

Penalties: 13

Points: 76

When Sam Tucker, Bristol's famous hooker, retired at the end of the 1930/31 season, the club was fortunate to acquire the services of his successor in the England team. Gordon Gregory made his international debut as a Taunton player against Ireland in February 1931, despite appearing in none of England's three trials that season. This was the first of 13 consecutive appearances as England's hooker, 10 as a Bristol player. Gregory had the added advantage of being a goalkicker, and he was successful with 2 conversions in England's 13-3 victory in Dublin in 1934. He tasted defeat in his first 5 internationals, including the 1932 game with South Africa. His first England victory was against Ireland in Dublin in 1932 and eventually he played in 6 international wins.

Having become the first player to be capped from the Taunton club, a club for which his father and two brothers also played, he joined Bristol at the start of the 1931/32 season, making his debut in the opening match against Cardiff. He made 22 appearances in his first season and won his first-team cap, having quickly established a reputation as a consistent forward with a talent for controlled dribbling in foot rushes. He held off all challenges for his position in the England team for the next three years.

Gordon Gregory was educated at Huish's Grammar School in Taunton, moving on to study agricultural science, first at Seale Haine College in Newton Abbot, then at Reading University, where he gained his BSc and captained the rugby team. He played for the Barbarians and for the combined Gloucestershire and Somerset team which lost to the 1931 South Africans at Bristol; in all he made 33 appearances for Somerset, gaining a county blazer in 1934 and captaining the side in 1932/33. Whilst playing for Bristol he was vice-principal of Somerset Farm Institute, Cannington, Bridgwater. He played briefly for Bath in 1932 but his final Bristol game was against Leicester in March 1934 during which he kicked his side's only points in a 5-3 defeat. His work then took him to London and he joined Blackheath. While he was with Blackheath he played in the Somerset team which lost the 1935 County final to Lancashire at Bath.

Although Gordon Gregory's Bristol career was relatively brief he was an established international throughout his time at the club and is remembered as one of Bristol's stars of the early 1930s.

Jack Gregory

Wing

Born: 22 June 1923

Career: 1949-54

Appearances: 129 games

Representative Honours: Gloucestershire, Barbarians, Western Counties, Army, England

Tries: 73

Drop Goals: 2

Points: 225

Jack Gregory was a member of the 1948 4x 100m relay team which won a silver medal at the London Olympics. The medals were briefly upgraded to gold when the winning American team was disqualified, but the winners were reinstated on appeal and the British runners had to be content with silver. Gregory's incredible speed was of great value to Bristol, whom he joined in 1949, and his record of 73 tries in 129 games is impressive.

Gregory was educated at St Andrew's College, Dublin, and Rydal School and played for Wanderers, Clifton and Blackheath as well as Bristol. As a Blackheath player, he won his only England cap in the 9-3 defeat against Wales at Cardiff in 1949. He was in the Army from 1941 to 1947 and during this time he courted controversy by playing rugby league while stationed at Huddersfield just after the war. He applied to play union again, but was initially banned by the RFU. The Army RU

appealed on his behalf and eventually he was reinstated, although he had to serve a year's ban until 1948.

Jack Gregory won his Bristol cap at the end of his first season and was vice-captain in 1951/52. During this season he played for Western Counties against South Africa and was Bristol's leading try-scorer, although his tally of 11 is evidence that the club had a poor season during which his talents were underused. At the end of the season, the club was invited to play in the Middlesex Sevens for the first time but Gregory was unable to play as he was training with the relay team for the Helsinki Olympics. This time he missed out on a medal, the team finishing fourth.

Gregory became Bristol captain in 1952 and held this office for two seasons. His try tally improved, partly due to the skillful cross-kicking of outside half Glyn Davies, and he and his opposite winger Keith Smith both scored 19 tries. During his second season of captaincy he led the try-scorers with 18 and captained Western Counties against the touring All Blacks. He was also a member of the Bristol squad which played in the first Snelling Sevens at Newport. He retired at the end of this season.

Jack Gregory played 28 games for Gloucestershire, appearing in the 1949 final defeat against Lancashire when he was still with Blackheath. He played twice for the Barbarians, but, despite receiving further trials, he was unable to add to his solitary England appearance.

Born: 19 October 1944

Career: 1970-74

Appearances: 108 games

Representative Honours: Durham, Gloucestershire, UAU, British Universities, Barbarians, Gloucestershire & Somerset XV, South & South West, Western Counties, England

Tries: 22

Points: 77

Charlie Hannaford was one of the most energetic players to have played for Bristol. Tall and fit, he played in seven county championship finals and had a long coaching career.

Born in Almondsbury and educated at Crypt School in Gloucester, Hannaford studied at Durham and Cambridge universities before becoming a teacher. He was an England schools Under-19 international and played regularly for Gloucester and occasionally for Old Cryptians when home from university. He also played for Durham City, Durham University, and represented Durham in the county championship on 20 occasions. Once the centre of an ineligibility controversy, he played for Durham in the 1965 and 1967 finals. He played for Rosslyn Park whilst at Cambridge, where he won a Blue in 1967, and remained a 'Park' player when rugby master at Sherborne School, where he succeeded Richard Sharp.

Hannaford joined Bristol when he took up an appointment at Clifton College and made his debut for the club at Cross Keys in September 1970. He had a highly successful season with Bristol, culminating in selection for England. He made a try-scoring debut against Wales in 1971 and toured Japan and the Far East with England later that year. He won 3 caps for England in total.

Hannaford was an athletic forward who dominated the tail of the line-out. He was particularly mobile and possessed good hands.

He developed a fearsome back-row partnership with Dave Rollitt, who moved to blind side to accommodate him.

A Barbarian, Hannaford played for Gloucestershire & Somerset against Fiji in 1970, the South and South West against the RFU President's XV in 1971, Western Counties against New Zealand in 1972, and in the South & South West side that defeated Australia in 1973. He was also a member of the Bristol team in the 1973 Cup final. Hannaford played for Gloucestershire in 5 successive county championship finals from 1970, including the 1972 triumph in which he scored a try, and the victory over Lancashire in 1974.

He left Bristol for New Zealand in 1974 shortly after the county final. He acted as player-coach for the Nae Nae club in Wellington and for Eastbourne RFC. He later returned to England and joined the staff at Millfield School. He played for the Tor club and then became player-coach for Cirencester when at Rendcomb College. He also coached Gloucestershire, and later became headmaster of Seaford College in West Sussex.

Charlie Hannaford recently retired, having coached at school or club level for nearly thirty years, and now lives in France.

Richard Harding

Scrum-half

Born: 29 August 1954

Career: 1973-91

Appearances: 395 games

Representative Honours: England Schools, Barbarians, Gloucestershire, Somerset, South & South West, England

Tries: 75

Points: 300

Scrum-half Richard Harding gained a special place in the hearts of England rugby followers in 1985 when he tackled French wing Patrick Esteve, preventing a certain try and saving his country from defeat. Esteve had already crossed the line at Twickenham, but delayed touching the ball down and as Harding tackled him he threw it forward. The game ended in a draw.

This was Harding's second international, following his debut against Romania a month earlier. He gained 12 caps in all, and was first choice scrum-half in the 1987 World Cup. With Nigel Melville and Richard Hill both attracting the selectors' attention Harding had to make the most of his chances, and he certainly did this against Ireland in 1988 when he replaced Melville at half time, inspiring a hitherto sluggish England to a 35-3 victory. Thereafter, Harding kept his place for the Millennium Challenge with Ireland, scoring his only international try, and he

ended his England career on the 1988 tour to Australia and Fiji. He played in all 3 internationals and was England captain in his final game, the 25-12 victory over Fiji.

Richard Harding played rugby at Park Grammar School, Swindon before going to Millfield, where he captained the school and played for England Schools. He played senior rugby for Bath and Somerset while still at Millfield and won Blues at St John's College, Cambridge in 1973 and 1974, playing for the university against the 1972 All Blacks. Harding joined Bristol in 1973, making his debut at Leicester. He and Alan Pearn vied for the Bristol scrum-half berth for the next couple of years before work took Harding to the Midlands, where he played one season for Moseley. He came into his own as Bristol's first choice when he returned to the club in 1978, impressing with his darting runs, superb passing and intelligent reading of a game.

Harding played most of his county rugby for his native Gloucestershire, numbering the victorious county finals of 1974, 1983 and 1984 amongst his 26 appearances. He played 7 games for local selections against tourists, once against Fiji, New Zealand and Romania, and 4 times against Australia, ending with the 26-10 win against the Wallabies at Bristol in 1988. He captained the division in the 1987 championship and played in all 3 of Bristol's cup finals of the 1980s. He finished playing in 1991, but he has remained involved in the game, coaching budding scrum-halves at Millfield and summarising at Bristol games for local radio.

Dick Hawkes
Second row

Born: 28 August 1924

Career: 1954-57

Appearances: 92 games

Representative Honours: Somerset, Barbarians, Leicestershire & East Midlands XV, East Midlands, England trialist

Tries: 9

Points: 27

Dick Hawkes, a strong second-row forward and a fine line-out jumper, only played three seasons with Bristol but was captain of the highly successful 1956/57 team, doing much to encourage the exciting style of play which was to reach its zenith in the John Blake era.

Hawkes joined the club from Northampton in 1954, winning his first-team cap at the end of the season, and after playing 30 matches in 1955/56 he led Bristol to a record of 33 victories from 42 games in his year of captaincy. This was a new club record for victories in a season, and in addition, the 573 points total was the club's best up to that time. Only 4 matches were lost away from home and Bristol gained its first ever double against Swansea as well as winning at both Llanelli and Newport. Hawkes' season of captaincy also saw the innovation of floodlit rugby at Bristol City's Ashton Gate ground and a fixture with a Romanian XV. Before the latter game he received a pennant from the visitors on behalf of the club. Hawkes, who had played for Somerset since arriving in Bristol, retired at the end of this memorable season.

During the Second World War Hawkes served in the Royal Tank Regiment. Having previously appeared for Yeovil, he played for Northampton from 1947, making 171 appearances. He played county rugby for East Midlands and was a member of the side which won the 1951 County Championship, beating Middlesex 10-0 at Northampton. He also appeared in the Leicestershire and East Midlands side which lost only 3-0 to the 1953 New Zealand tourists. The All Blacks were very impressed with his line-out play and veteran New Zealand journalist, Winston McCarthy dubbed him the best line-out forward the tourists had encountered. Hawkes faced the tourists again in the final match of the tour as one of two uncapped players in the Barbarians side which lost 19-5 at Cardiff. Recognising the potential threat of Hawkes, the New Zealanders chose their great forward, 'Tiny' White, to jump against him. White played brilliantly, depriving Hawkes and his team of much valuable ball.

Although never receiving the ultimate accolade of an England cap, Dick Hawkes was regularly in the minds of the selectors and he played in a total of 6 international trials from 1949 to 1954. He probably came closest to a cap in 1953/54 when he followed his game for the Probables with an appearance for England against the Rest in the final trial. Unfortunately, England lost this game 8-6 and Hawkes was never to get another trial, but he continued to enjoy his rugby and remains a staunch advocate of the amateur ethos.

David Hazell

Prop

Born: 23 April 1931

Career: 1956-64

Appearances: 241 games

Representative Honours: Barbarians, Leicestershire, Somerset, English Universities, Midland Counties, England

Tries: 10

Conversions: 135

Penalties: 61

Points: 483

David Hazell provided valuable experience and stability to the Bristol front row during the late 1950s and early 1960s. An expert scrummager, he was also a highly proficient goal kicker. Born on St George's Day, he caused confusion, and probably panic, with his initials. David St George Hazell was abbreviated to D. St G. Hazell causing many to believe he was a detective sergeant!

Educated at Taunton School, he played rugby for the school team, which he captained. A talented sportsman, he also played cricket for Somerset Colts. He studied at Loughborough Colleges and later became a teacher. Whilst at Loughborough Hazell represented English Universities and played for them in Italy. He had a lucky escape as the aircraft he had flown in crashed on its return flight. He played for Loughborough and Leicester, and continued to play for the Tigers when teaching in Nottingham. He also played county rugby for Leicestershire.

Hazell was an unusual player. At a time when props pushed and shoved in a scrum and did little else, Hazell provided considerable added value. He was technically a very solid scrummager, but was particularly mobile and contributed much to play in the open. Perhaps most remarkable of all was his sublime goal kicking. During his four seasons

at Leicester he broke the points scoring record twice.

He played throughout the 1955 Five Nations championship for England, enjoying an impressive debut in the match against Wales and kicking the winning goal in victory over Scotland. He won 4 caps in all, played for Midland Counties against New Zealand in 1953 and also represented the Barbarians.

Hazell's rugby career was severely hampered by a shattering knee injury suffered at the 1956 end-of-season Leicester sevens. He missed virtually all the following season, during which he changed jobs and returned to the West Country. He joined Bristol at the end of 1956/57, but managed to injure his knee again and missed the beginning of the following season.

Hazell took over the place-kicking duties at Bristol when Gordon Cripps retired. He was Bristol's vice-captain for the 1959/60 and 1963/64 seasons. He captained Somerset, for whom he played regularly, and also led Western Counties against New Zealand in 1963.

He left Bristol at the end of the 1963/64 season when he found travelling from Taunton excessive, and played occasionally for a Somerset veterans team. David Hazell continued his involvement in rugby as master in charge of rugby, and cricket, at his old school, Taunton, until his retirement.

Bob Hesford

Born: 26 March 1953

Career: 1978-85

Appearances: 182 games

Representative Honours: Barbarians, Gloucestershire, South & South West, England U23, England

Tries: 53

Points: 212

Bob Hesford was one third of the dynamic back row of the early 1980s. His talents combined with those of Mike Rafter and Peter Polledri to provide the catalyst to unparalleled success.

Born in Blackpool, Hesford was educated at Arnold School, Blackpool, and Durham University. His father played in goal for Huddersfield in the 1938 FA Cup final and his brother Iain, also a goalkeeper, represented England Under-21 and played for Blackpool, Sunderland and South China. A further brother, Steve, was a leading rugby league player with Warrington. However, Bob Hesford played rugby union and, although not winning any significant schoolboy honours, he represented Durham University before becoming a teacher. He played a season for Wasps when working in London before heading to Zambia for three years where he met Bill Redwood and played rugby in Lusaka, for an ex-pats team. When Hesford returned to England he took up an appointment in Bristol. He played for Old Colstonians before being invited to join Bristol. He made his debut at Moseley in December 1978 and soon became a permanent fixture in the side.

Hesford was a very powerful number eight with excellent footballing skills. He was particularly successful at picking up and driving from the back of a scrum, and linked seamlessly with Rafter and Polledri to form a perfectly balanced unit.

A try-scorer in the 1983 Cup Final triumph, Hesford played for the South & South West Division against Australia in 1981 and 1984, against Fiji in 1982 and Romania in 1985. He was a regular Gloucestershire player and also played for England Under-23 and the Barbarians.

An England squad member, he won his first international cap against Scotland in 1981 as a replacement for Nick Jeavons. At the end of the season he toured Argentina and played three times for England the following season. He played throughout the 1985 Five Nations championship and made 10 international appearances in all. He toured New Zealand with England at the end of the season and was chosen as captain for the match against Otago. Having achieved the accolade of captaining his country, Hesford retired after the game.

Hesford served on the Bristol committee and helped Mike Rafter with coaching duties before becoming club coach himself and guiding play during the club's successful centenary season. He later coached at Whitehall and Barton Hill, rejecting approaches from bigger clubs because he wished to continue teaching.

Bob Hesford is currently the coach of Dings Crusaders and is a special needs teacher at Vinney Green Secure Unit.

Alistair Hignell

Full-back

Born: 4 September 1955

Career: 1974-80

Appearances: 58 games

Representative Honours: England Schools, Barbarians, Gloucestershire, England

Tries: 14

Conversions: 34

Penalties: 28

Points: 208

Alastair Hignell won Cambridge Blues at rugby and cricket for 4 consecutive years, captaining his university at both sports. He played county cricket for Gloucestershire, scoring 7 centuries, and won 14 England rugby caps as a courageous full-back.

His international debut was in the second test of England's tour of Australia in 1975 when the visitors lost 30-21. England gained revenge in 1976 when Australia lost 23-6 at Twickenham, Hignell contributing 1 conversion and 3 penalties to the winning total. He played in 3 more 1976 internationals, kicking three penalties against Wales, and appeared in all championship games the following year. His kicking let him down in a narrow home defeat against France, but he redeemed himself with an outstanding performance in Cardiff, when his 3 penalties were the only England scores in a 14-9 loss. He kicked 2 penalties when Wales won at Twickenham in 1978, becoming the only Englishman to score against Wales between 1976 and 1978.

A hamstring injury forced Hignell to miss the game against Scotland, but he had one more full championship season in 1979. Injured again in 1980, he stopped playing to concentrate on his cricket. Alastair Hignell

learned his rugby at Denstone College in Staffordshire, where he played at scrum-half and captained the school XV. He also captained England Schools and made his Bristol debut at Pontypool in March 1974. He briefly displaced Alan Pearn as first choice scrum-half towards the end of the season. Going up to Fitzwilliam College, Cambridge, he found another Bristol player, Richard Harding, was the established varsity scrum-half, and he switched to full-back. He played little for Bristol during the ensuing years, but returned when he started to teach at Bristol Cathedral School.

His time at Cambridge, plus various injuries, meant that Alastair Hignell only played 58 times for Bristol. Perhaps his most memorable game in a Bristol shirt was a thrilling 17-17 draw with Cardiff at the Arms Park in September 1979. Hignell moved to outside half when David Sorrell was injured and his daring attacking play in the closing stages set up 2 late tries which brought Bristol back from a 17-9 deficit.

Alastair Hignell played 4 games for the Barbarians and 3 championship matches for Gloucestershire, each in a different position. He was at outside half against Hertfordshire in 1975, full-back against Oxfordshire in 1979 and centre in the 1980 final. Now involved in broadcasting, he is fighting a brave battle against multiple sclerosis and has won deserved admiration for his courage.

Fred Hill
Hooker

Born: 17 January 1917

Died: 3 November 1997

Career: 1949-50

Appearances: 141 matches

Representative Honours: Gloucestershire, Gloucestershire & Somerset XV, England 'Victory' internationalist

Tries: 3

Points: 9

Fred Hill, who was Bristol's first post-Second World War hooker, achieved fame in rugby despite losing an eye as an eighteen-year-old in a skating accident at the Coliseum in Park Row. He first came to prominence in the wartime Bristol Supporters' team, although Private Fred Hill sometimes appeared on the team sheet as a prop forward. He had previously made a few pre-war appearances for Bristol United, making his debut against Sidmouth in 1937.

After the war Hill was an automatic choice for Bristol, and this expert hooker played in the opening game against Stroud. He played in more games than any other forward during the season and also appeared for England in two of the so-called 'Victory Internationals' which were staged in place of the normal round of championship games. He made his debut against Scotland at Twickenham, sharing in a 12-8 win, but he was not so fortunate when the return fixture was played at Murrayfield, Scotland enjoying a runaway 27-0 victory. Unfortunately for Hill, these games were not deemed worthy of full international status and caps were not awarded. He played in 3 trials the following season, each time on the losing side, and he was never to win the cap his ability deserved.

Despite his tantalising bad luck in the 1946/47 trials, the season as a whole was still memorable for Hill, as Gloucestershire reached the County final, qualifying to play

Lancashire at Blundellsands. The county looked set to gain the title when they held their hosts to an 8-8 draw, but lost the replay at Gloucester, 14-3. This was the first of two near misses during Hill's county career. He also played in the 1949 final, again at Blundellsands, which Lancashire won 9-3. In all he made 25 Gloucestershire appearances.

In 1947/48, Fred Hill led the Bristol appearances with 39 starts out of a possible 42. He was awarded his club blazer, having previously won his cap at the end of 1945/46. He played another full season in 1948/49, but only appeared in 16 games the following year. Thereafter he joined Bath, where he was once credited with a pushover try whilst off the field injured!

Fred Hill, who also played for the St Agnes and Broad Plain clubs plus Broughton Park during the war, appeared for the Army against both the other services in 1946. He was also in the combined Gloucestershire and Somerset XV which played the Kiwis. A carpenter, he constructed a special kitchen table which was the correct height for hooking practice. He taught his son Harvey, a Bristol player in later years, to hook by heeling the ball into the gas oven.

Simon Hogg
Centre/Outside half

Born: 27 October 1960

Career: 1982-91

Appearances: 222 games

Representative Honours: Gloucestershire, Devon, England Students, England U23

Tries: 45

Conversions: 191

Penalties: 133

Drop Goals: 24

Points: 1,033

Simon Hogg, an immensely popular centre, full-back and outside half, was one of Bristol's finest backs of the 1980s. His approach to rugby was Corinthian and non-conformist, but he was a committed sharer in the triumphs of the decade and was often a match winner.

Hogg attended Bristol Grammar School where he appeared for Bristol and Gloucestershire Schools and played in an England Schools trial. He also acted as first XV captain when Andy Dun was injured. He continued his education at Exeter University, where he captained the first team, played for England Students and Devon, and appeared in two UAU finals. Both ended in narrow defeats to Durham, the latter because Durham scored the only try in a drawn game. He then went to teach at Taunton School.

Simon Hogg made his Bristol debut on the wing at Bedford in January 1982, but the following season he became Ralph Knibbs' regular centre partner. They were selected together for Gloucestershire as part of an all-Bristol back division in the 1983 County final. This was Hogg's championship debut for Gloucestershire and he shared in a fine victory, as he did the following season when he was a try-scorer in the Twickenham triumph over Somerset.

Hogg crowned the 1982/83 season by scoring a superb try in Bristol's cup final win against Leicester. He was not so fortunate in his other final appearances, appearing in the defeats of 1984 and 1988. In the latter game he played at outside half and had what appeared to be a good drop goal disallowed.

Hogg played 36 of Bristol's games in 1983/84, winning his club cap and playing for England Under-23s. He won his Bristol blazer in 1987. At the start of Bristol's centenary year, he found himself out of favour and turned out for Old Bristolians before being recalled at outside half for the game with the Barbarians in October. He scored the equalising try in the final minute and went on to feature strongly in a run of 21 consecutive victories. At the end of the season he skippered the Bristol seven which lost the Middlesex final to Harlequins. A sevens expert, he also appeared for a Bristol University select squad in the Safari Sevens in Kenya.

Simon Hogg, who was Andy Dun's vice-captain in 1989/90, left Bristol in 1991 and embarked on a rewarding decade of rugby with Clifton, during which he broke the club record for points in a season and master-minded Clifton's first victory against Bristol for nearly forty years. Still at Taunton School, Simon Hogg also coaches Devon club Withycombe.

Archie Hore

Second row

Born: Unknown

Died: Unknown

Career: 1920-29

Appearances: 272 games

Representative Honours: Gloucestershire

Tries: 22

Conversions: 140

Penalties: 40

Points: 466

Archie Hore was Bristol's principal goal kicker during the mid 1920s, reaching his peak in the 1927/28 season when his grand total of 131 was made up of 43 conversions, 14 penalties and a solitary try. This was one of the club's very best seasons and Hore, a forward who usually packed down in the second row, appeared in 37 of the 42 games played, a figure only matched by full-back Tom Brown. Bristol only lost once at home and no side defeated the club twice.

Archie Hore was a regular in the Bristol pack for most of the decade, making his debut against Risca at the start of 1920/21 and winning his cap at the end of that season. Originally a back, he learned the game at Fairfield School and then played for local sides North Street Old Boys and Bristol Saracens. During the First World War he was sent to the Near East and while he was there he represented Palestine in a game against Egypt and also excelled at soccer, hockey and boxing. He played in the opening game on the Memorial Ground, won his club blazer at the end of 1922/23 and took part in Bristol's first-ever victory at Swansea, kicking a conversion in the 8-3 win in 1925. He also kicked a goal when Bristol travelled to France and defeated Cognac 8-6.

Gloucestershire won the County Championship for 3 successive seasons in the early 1920s, and Hore appeared in the last of these triumphs, when North Midlands were beaten 19-0 at Villa Park in 1922. He was not so fortunate three years later when he was a member of the team which lost the 1925 final at home to Leicestershire. Earlier that season he played in the Gloucestershire side which lost only 6-0 to the invincible Second All Blacks. The second half of this game, played in atrocious conditions at Gloucester, saw the home pack dominating for long periods, and the New Zealanders had to fight hard to prevent their line being crossed.

Archie Hore carried on playing up to 1928/29 and he made his final appearance against Bradford on Easter Tuesday, kicking a conversion in a 23-0 victory. Bristol's *Jubilee Book* states that he was greatly missed, but he seems to have been forgotten by subsequent generations and he has rarely received the recognition merited by his career statistics. These stand as evidence of his value to the exciting and successful Bristol team of this era.

Roger Hosen
Full-back

Born: 12 June 1933

Career: 1966-69

Appearances: 48 games

Representative Honours: Barbarians, Cornwall, Hampshire, Midlands, England

Tries: 1

Conversions: 41

Penalties: 54

Drop Goals: 4

Points: 259

Roger Hosen was one of the greatest goal kickers the game has ever seen. A multi-talented sportsman, he was Bristol's full-back for three seasons and he once held the Five Nations points-scoring record.

Educated at Falmouth Grammar School and Loughborough Colleges, Hosen played for several clubs – Penryn, Plymouth Albion, Cheltenham, Wasps, Neath and Northampton – before joining Bristol in time for the 1966/67 season. A master at Cheltenham College, he found it impossible to continue playing for Northampton. Instead of rejoining Cheltenham, for whom he had played when on National Service at RAF Innsworth, he joined Bristol. Life at Bristol was good fun for Hosen. Supremely fit, he had learnt the skill of quality training at Loughborough and was well suited to Bristol's attack-orientated approach to the game. He was versatile, consistent and a very reliable player. A solid tackler who possessed an almost magnetic attraction to the high ball, it was his goal-kicking which was most remarkable. Experts believed he could kick a rugby ball further than anyone else in England.

Whilst at Loughborough Hosen played centre for Midland Counties against New Zealand in 1953. He played in a trial match for England in 1954 at centre but had to wait nearly ten years before gaining his first England cap. He was selected for England's first overseas tour, to New Zealand and Australia in 1963, and made his debut against the All Blacks in Auckland. He caught the eye of prominent journalists who were surprised that England had a full-back seemingly in the New Zealand mould. He was declared one of the Five Players of the Year in New Zealand, a rare honour for a British player.

When he returned he was capped on the wing by England. Mysteriously dropped, he later returned to the England side as a Bristol player and won the last of his ten caps against Wales in 1967. He scored 38 points in the 1967 international championship, at the time a record for the tournament. Hosen left Bristol at the end of the 1968/69 season when commitments at Cheltenham College became greater. He rejoined the Cheltenham club and played for them for a couple of seasons. A proud Cornishman, Hosen represented the Duchy on 54 occasions, and captained the side. He also captained Cornwall at cricket and played cricket for the Minor Counties.

Roger Hosen, the siege-gun kicker who was one of the first to apply science and organisation to his personal training and fitness, later retired from teaching and became a publican in Cornwall.

Paul Hull
Full-back

Born: 17 May 1968

Career: 1987-99

Appearances: 289 games

Representative Honours: England Colts, U19, U21, A, England 7's, Barbarians, Combined Services, South West Division, England

Tries: 61

Conversions: 91

Penalties: 59

Drop Goals: 3

Points: 649

Paul Hull is one of the most versatile and loyal players to have played for Bristol. A dazzling runner, he was an England international and now has a key role in the club's future.

A multi-talented sportsman, Hull had soccer trials with Southampton but considered he was more likely to play sport for England through rugby. He played for Milton Keynes when he was seventeen, and joined the Royal Air Force where he became a physical training instructor.

An England Colts international, Hull played briefly for Coventry when stationed at RAF Cosford before being posted to RAF Lyneham and joining Bristol. He played once for Bristol United in 1986/87 and made his first-team debut as a replacement against Newport in December 1987.

Hull quickly developed into a highly effective attacker for Bristol, possessing the ability to swerve at top speed. He was predominantly a full-back and his incursions into the line at pace frequently broke defensive formations, usually to the benefit of his try-scoring wingers.

He played regularly for the RAF, and for Combined Services teams that played touring sides. He was also a Barbarian and played for the South West Division, which he later captained. Capped at Under-19 and Under-21 level, Hull played for England A in 1989, and captained the 1995 A tour to Australia and Fiji. He played against the 1993 All Blacks on 4 occasions, including Emerging England. Hull 'emerged' and toured South Africa with England in 1994. He played in both internationals and returned with his reputation enhanced. He played in the 1994 autumn internationals but was injured and lost his place. Although remaining on the fringe of the squad he was never capped again.

Hull had attractive offers to join many leading English clubs, plus Castleford and Warrington rugby league sides but he remained loyal to Bristol. He played at outside half, centre and wing when required and his commendable commitment to the club made him the most popular of players. An accomplished goal kicker, Hull started a record 149 league games for Bristol. He was vice-captain for four seasons before becoming captain for 1995/96, the highlight of his Bristol career. His last Bristol game was against Cardiff in August 1999. He injured his Achilles and was forced to retire a few months later.

Currently the manager of the Bristol rugby academy, Hull coached the successful Under-21 teams which won their league 3 seasons in a row. Paul Hull is also the assistant coach to the current Bristol squad.

Wallace Jarman

Forward

Born: 15 July 1872

Died: September 1950

Career: 1900-05*

Appearances: 50 games*

Representative Honours: Gloucestershire, The South, England, British Team

Tries: 1*

Points: 3*

* additional appearances and points prior to 1900

Wallace Jarman was Bristol's first ever international player, gaining his cap for England as a forward in the game against Wales on 6 January 1900. This was in the pre-Twickenham era when clubs around the country lobbied the English Rugby Union for the privilege of staging international matches. The Bristol committee had made strenuous efforts to have the game staged at the County Ground, but Gloucester was the chosen venue and it was at Kingsholm that Jarman created club history. This was an extraordinary game in which England awarded no less than 13 new caps, including the entire pack. Unfortunately for Jarman, Wales won 13-3 and he and a number of others were dropped for the following game. This caused some dissatisfaction in the Bristol area, especially as it was generally agreed that Jarman had played well. The Bristol committee seriously considered making an official protest, and the minutes of the time refer to the ERU executive as being 'quite hopeless'. Sadly, this was to be Jarman's only cap.

Irrespective of his special place of honour as the club's first international, Wallace Jarman deserves to be remembered as one of the major figures in Bristol's early years. He was educated at Merchant Venturers School, and joined Bristol from the Knowle club, then a dominant force in local rugby. He received his Bristol cap at the end of the 1893/94 season, and was appointed captain in 1896/97. Jarman held this office for 5 seasons, a record only equalled in more recent times by Derek Eves. It was under his leadership that Bristol gained its first victory over Newport, winning 8-5 in January 1900, just a week after Jarman's solitary international. He relinquished the captaincy at the end of the 1900/01 season, but continued to play, though less regularly, up to 1905, making his final appearance against Percy Park in April of that year. By then he was already Bristol's chairman, an office he held from 1902 to 1909.

Bristol's *Jubilee Book* provides us with a superb thumbnail sketch of Jarman: 'Puritan in upbringing and habit he was a fine character, full of humour and kindliness, yet a veritable Spartan where physical fitness counted.' He was greatly valued by his fellow club members, and was made a life member of the club in 1901. He was also awarded a special dinner when he was selected for the British team which toured Australia in 1899. This was by no means a fully representative side as many of the party were, like Jarman,

uncapped at the time, and twelve of the tourists, including the captain, were never capped by their countries. Australia won the first test of this series, but the British team won the remaining 3, and Jarman had the honour of playing in all 4 tests. It was to be ninety years before another British team made an exclusive tour of Australia.

It says much for Wallace Jarman's stamina, enthusiasm and ability that he was able to return from Australia and go straight into a new season as his club's captain, playing rugby worthy of international selection in the process. Other honours to come his way during his career included an appearance for The South against The North in 1899 and a total of 28 caps for Gloucestershire.

Wallace Jarman emigrated to Canada in 1920, and worked for Cadbury-Fry in Alberta for many years. He made a brief return to Bristol in 1936 and his old playing contemporaries held a dinner for him at the Royal Hotel. He continued to live in Canada after his retirement and died in Vancouver in 1950.

Billy Johnston

Full-back

Born: 1887

Died: c. 1939

Career: 1906-20

Appearances: 133

Representative Honours: Gloucestershire, England

Tries: 3

Conversions: 49

Penalties: 12

Drop Goals: 4

Points: 159

Billy Johnston was England's premier full-back in the years immediately prior to the First World War. Despite being of Irish descent, he made 16 appearances for England, and his total of caps was England's record for a full-back until it was beaten by Bob Hiller in 1971.

Johnston made his international debut against Wales in 1910. This was the first international played at Twickenham and brought England a long overdue victory against a country that had dominated the international scene for much of the previous decade. Johnston retained his place for the game with Ireland but was unable to travel to France for England's match there. He returned to the side for the final match of the season against Scotland. S.H. Williams of Newport took Johnston's place for the 1911 internationals but retired at the end of the season. Thereafter Johnston was the number one choice, appearing in all the championship games up to the war as well as the match against the 1912 South Africans. England won the Grand Slam in 1913 and 1914 and Johnston was only on the losing side twice as an England player.

Johnston was educated at Colston's School and first appeared for Bristol in 1906. He captained the team during the 1909/10 season and stepped in to skipper the side again when Maurice Neale unexpectedly left after a month of the 1911/12 campaign. Johnston retained the captaincy for the rest of that season and for the following one as well.

Johnston was not renowned for his pace but various sources pay tribute to his safe catching, his kicking and his tackling. His attributes are perhaps best described by veteran Welsh journalist W.J.T. Collins, who, in his *Rugby Reminiscences,* states that Johnston was: 'Sound in judgement, calm, unflurried, with a sense of position which made it seem as if opponents were deliberately kicking to him.'

As well as appearing in the first Twickenham international, Johnston was involved in another first when he played in the Gloucestershire side which defeated Yorkshire 23-0 at Gloucester in 1910 to win the county's first championship. He played 20 games for Gloucestershire, including the 1912 match against South Africa, and also played for the combined Bristol and Clifton team against the 1908 Australian tourists. He did not return to rugby after the war, but was persuaded out of retirement to face Newport in 1920. Unfortunately, he received a serious rib injury in this game and a fine career ended on a sad note.

Ralph Knibbs

Centre

Born: 3 August 1964

Career: 1982-96

Appearances: 436 games

Representative Honours: Gloucestershire, England U23, England sevens, England Squad, South West Division

Tries: 123

Conversions: 11

Penalties: 8

Drop Goals: 6

Points: 573

Ralph Knibbs was one of the most gifted and exciting backs ever to play for Bristol. Chiefly a centre, although he also appeared as a winger and full-back, he made a sensational first-team debut at the age of seventeen, scoring with his first touch of the ball in the home victory over Pontypridd in March 1982. Bristol, smarting after a shock cup defeat against Liverpool, embarked on a winning run of fourteen matches and Knibbs, who had previously appeared for both Bristol Colts and Bristol United during the season, played in all but the last of these. He did not taste defeat in a Bristol first-team game until the following season. He quickly became a favourite with the Bristol supporters, scoring some wonderful tries, often from seemingly impossible positions. His jinking, dummying, unusual angles of running and sheer speed, coupled with skills learned as a basketball player, made him a difficult and unorthodox opponent, particularly in his early years. He could also kick and drop goals when called upon, yet he never achieved the full England cap that his talents deserved.

Knibbs was educated at Whitefield comprehensive school and Brunel College and first played in Bristol's Colts team in 1980/81, scoring 19 tries in 23 games and kicking many

goals. By then he had already played for Bristol Schools at Under-14 and Under-16 level, and had also featured in an England Schools' trial. He played for Southwest Colts during his second season of colts rugby. Following his brilliant start in the Bristol first team, he appeared in 35 games during 1982/83, winning his cap. He played in the victorious 1983 cup final as an eighteen year old and was also a member of Gloucestershire's County Championship winning side. At the end of the season he was selected for the England Under 23 tour of Romania.

1983/84 was another memorable season for Knibbs, again culminating in an Under-23 tour, this time to Spain. He tasted cup final defeat at Twickenham with Bristol, but scored one of Gloucestershire's tries in the runaway County final success against Somerset. His club blazer and more England Under 23 rugby followed in 1984/85 and he led Bristol's appearances with 40 games in 1985/86. In the meantime, he had turned down a chance to tour South Africa with England in 1984, making an admirable moral stand against the evils of apartheid. In a newspaper interview at the time Knibbs, while admitting that he was sorry not to have the chance to represent his country, stated: 'I don't see how I could justify going to South Africa, therefore appearing to condone apartheid.'

Over the next few seasons Knibbs trained with both the England B and full England squads, but he continually missed out on international selection. He was sounded out on his availability for England's tour to Australia in 1988, but this time work commitments prevented him from going. He did, however, star for the England seven which lost the final of the Sport Aid tournament to New Zealand in Cardiff in 1986 and he later represented his country in the Dubai Sevens. He also played for the Penguins seven which represented England at the Hong Kong Sevens, reaching the semi-finals in 1987.

Knibbs, who excelled at athletics and American football as well as the aforementioned basketball, continued to play regularly for Bristol in the late 1980s. He appeared more than any other back in 1986/87 and was vice-captain and leading appearance maker during the centenary year. He was a member of the team which lost the 1988 cup final to Harlequins and was back at Twickenham a week later to play for Bristol in the Middlesex Sevens. Knibbs scored a try in an exciting final against Harlequins, but again ended up on the losing side.

With the rise of divisional rugby, Knibbs became a regular member of the South West squad and in 1988/89 he appeared on the wing for the division against both Australia and the USA. He topped Bristol's appearances yet again in 1989/90 but was injured the following season and only played 17 matches. Thereafter he played 3 further full seasons before his first-team opportunities began to decline. His final first-team season was 1995/96 and his last game was at full-back against West Hartlepool in May.

Ralph Knibbs captained Bristol United during 1996/97 and then became part of the exodus of Bristol players to Coventry where he linked up with director of rugby, Derek Eves, and became coach. He then returned to Bristol to captain Clifton. In three seasons, he missed just 1 league game out of 78 played and provided much needed experience at the club. In 2001 he finally ended his lengthy playing career, a career which did not see the total fulfilment of its early promise in terms of international recognition, but which nevertheless brought pleasure and excitement to many. Ralph Knibbs was a genuine sportsman and a true Bristol great.

Peter Knight
Wing/Full-back

Born: 7 October 1947

Career: 1966-75

Appearances: 104 games

Representative Honours: Gloucestershire, Western Counties, England & Wales XV, England

Tries: 51

Points: 196

Peter Knight was one of Bristol's most gifted footballers. Possessing blistering pace and perfect balance he played for Bristol and England at full-back and on the wing. Educated at Bristol Cathedral School, he was introduced to rugby by former Bristol player Eric Blackman, whose enthusiasm was infectious. Knight was given an appreciation of all positions in the backs and became determined to play for England.

Knight played for Bristol United aged just sixteen and studied at St Luke's College and Durham University, playing for Bristol when on vacation. A stout tackler and deadly finisher, Knight was first able to play regularly for Bristol in 1971/72. He hit a rich vein of form at the start of the season and scored two tries in a remarkable 38-4 victory at Swansea. By the end of the season he had played for England against France and Scotland, and been chosen to tour South Africa. England achieved a notable test victory there, in which Alan Morley scored a try. Knight, playing on the other wing, only touched the ball once in play.

His talents were more evident in the abbreviated game of sevens. He was a member of the St Luke's team which won the Middlesex Sevens in 1969, and he was also a Westbury Harrier, highly rated nationally at the triple jump. Knight played for the combined counties against South Africa in 1969, Fiji in 1970 and New Zealand in 1972, and was a regular Gloucestershire player. He played on the wing for England & Wales against Scotland & Ireland in 1972.

Bristol reached the 1973 RFU Cup final at the end of a run which included a dramatic semi-final victory over a confident London Welsh. Knight scored a dazzling try, which saw him round J.P.R. Williams to score in their 18-15 victory. He toured New Zealand with England the following summer, but found his appetite for rugby had waned. He was at the top of his game and had achieved all he had set out to do, but found it difficult to see how his career could continue. Hence, he retired after the first game of the 1974/75 season, at Redruth, aged twenty-six.

Formerly a teacher at Sherborne School, Knight took up an appointment as head of PE at Clifton College. He worked there for twelve years before teaching the children of diplomats at the British School of Brussels in Belgium. He then studied theology at Trinity College in Bristol and was ordained as a priest in 1992. Peter Knight is now a clergyman in Swindon.

Bert Macdonald

Second row

Born: 10 January 1923

Career: 1948-61

Appearances: 344 games

Representative Honours: Gloucestershire, Western Counties, Scottish trial

Tries: 39

Points: 117

Bert Macdonald, a long-serving second row or number eight forward, was one of the greatest captains in Bristol's history and once held the club record for appearances. Remarkably, he played no rugby in his early years, being brought up in a soccer area in Scotland, yet at his peak he was good enough to appear in a Scottish trial and was considered unfortunate not to gain full international recognition.

Macdonald was in the RAF during the Second World War, training as a navigator in South Africa. After the war he continued his interest in soccer, playing as a goalkeeper for Shell Mex. He started his rugby with Avonmouth Old Boys and was spotted by Bristol's Tom Mahoney playing in an exhibition game and invited to try his luck at the Memorial Ground. He made his United debut

in 1948, and played 5 first-team games in his initial season. He was awarded his United cap at the end of the season and his first-team cap a year later, having established himself in the Bristol pack. A strong, well-built player, he soon attracted the attention of the Gloucestershire selectors, and was also chosen for the Western Counties side which lost to the 1951 South Africans. He won his club blazer at the end of 1951/52 and played in thirty or more games during this and the subsequent two seasons.

Macdonald's Scottish trial came in December 1953 when he played for the Blues against the Whites at Murrayfield. His team won the game 8-3, but he was not called up for a trial again and was perhaps unfortunate that he was based too far away for the Scottish selectors to monitor his progress regularly. However, Scotland's loss was definitely Bristol's gain and he was appointed club captain for 1954/55. During the season he played in 38 of Bristol's 40 games and more importantly was instrumental in implementing important changes in the club's style of play. In January 1955 Bristol lost 38-0 to a weakened Cardiff side and Macdonald announced to a subdued dressing room that changes would have to be made. With the full backing of the committee, he began to introduce better organised training and a more tactical approach to games. The club already had a big pack of ball-winning forwards and these were now encouraged to run and pass with the backs. The changes were gradual, but only five more games were lost during the season and Macdonald's leadership and example paved the way for the later glories of the John Blake era.

The new system really paid dividends in 1955/56, when Bristol, still under Macdonald's leadership, equalled the club record of 31 wins in a season. There was only 1 home defeat and Macdonald, who appeared in 33 matches, had the satisfaction of seeing his side gain a revenge victory over Cardiff. He was a major figure in Bristol's successes under Dick Hawkes in 1956/57 and was then vice-captain to Blake at the start of his wonderful period of leadership. He was a great influence on the forwards during this season and ensured that the fifteen-man game was maintained and enjoyed.

Bert Macdonald played two more full seasons for Bristol, sharing in the fun of rugby under Blake. In 1959/60 he passed Fred Coventry's longstanding club and first-team appearance records and then stepped down to captain Bristol United in 1960/61. Having led the first team with such success, he proceeded to influence the younger players of the club and the result was a record-breaking season. United won more games and scored more points than ever before. Only three matches were lost and the team's defence was so successful that a mere 25 tries were conceded. Macdonald retired from playing at the end of this season.

Bert Macdonald, whose brother Ian was also a Bristol player, played a total of 20 games for Gloucestershire. In addition to his aforementioned appearance against South Africa, he was a member of the Western Counties team which defeated Australia at Bristol in 1957. He moved to London in the 1960s, but in an effort to maintain links with his old club he helped to found the London-Bristol Rugby Society. This society was founded on 11 September 1964 and, under Macdonald's chairmanship, was successful for many years in providing a focal point for former players in

London and supporters coming to watch Bristol's matches in the capital. Meetings were held at The Cock Tavern, which was run by former Bristol player Doug Evans and there was often a dinner when Bristol played in London.

Although still based in London, Bert Macdonald continues to watch Bristol when he can, often in the company of his friend Derek Neate. Like Neate, he is remembered as one of Bristol's true greats, both as a player and a leader.

Lloyd Mathias
Forward

Born: 1878

Died: 21 November 1940

Career: 1900-09

Appearances: 186 games*

Representative Honours: Gloucestershire, England

Tries: 20*

Points: 60*

* additional appearances and points prior to 1900

J. Lloyd Mathias, a forward in the days before specialised positions, won 4 England caps during 1905/06, finishing on the losing side each time. His international debut was against Wales at Cardiff, the home team winning 25-0. He then appeared in the 17-3 defeat against Ireland at Cork, in which England's preparations were not helped by the Rugby Football Union's insistence that the players travel in third class railway coaches between Dublin and Cork. Mathias had no better luck in his final two internationals – an 8-0 defeat against Scotland and the game against New Zealand, which England lost 15-0.

Lloyd Mathias is one of those players whose early career is not covered by club statistics. He played 186 games between 1900 and 1909, but he certainly played before then as he received his first-team cap at the end of the 1899/1900 season and his second XV cap in 1896/97.

Mathias was appointed first-team captain in 1901/02 and held the position for two seasons. In his fourth match in charge, Bristol beat Cardiff for the first time, winning 3-0 at the County Ground. During this season, Mathias played for The Rest of the South against London Universities. Gloucestershire reached the County Final for the first time in 1902 and Mathias was in the side which lost 9-3 to Durham at Gloucester. He made a total of 28 county appearances. Business prevented him from devoting much time to the captaincy in 1902/03, but he played for The Rest of England and was first reserve for England against Scotland.

Mathias played for Gloucestershire against the 1906 South Africans and also appeared for Bristol against New Zealand in 1905. The New Zealanders lost only 1 game out of 32 and were years ahead of English teams in terms of tactics and fitness. At the end of the tour, *The Daily Mail* published a review of the tour entitled 'Why the All Blacks Triumphed'. Mathias contributed a brief article to this publication, reflecting on Bristol's 41-0 defeat in which he commented: 'Forty-one points is a goodly number, and our only consolation is that they did not cross our line so often as they did against Devon and Cornwall.' He concluded his piece with the honest assessment that: 'Compared with our guests, we have a tremendous lot to learn in rugby football.'

The Bristol club expressed its appreciation of John Lloyd Mathias's loyal service by making him an honorary life member in 1912.

Norman Moore
Forward

Born: 1877

Died: 8 March 1938

Career: 1901-10

Appearances: 215 games

Representative Honours: Gloucestershire, Somerset, England

Tries: 14

Conversions: 40

Penalties: 8

Drop Goals: 1

Points: 150

Norman Moore, a heavyweight forward, won three England caps in 1904. He made his international debut in an exciting 14-14 draw with Wales at Leicester, a game in which the England pack was dominant. He retained his place for the 19-0 victory over Ireland at Blackheath and scored a try in each half, thus becoming the first Bristol player to score in an international. His final cap was at Inverleith against Scotland, a match which the Scots won 6-3.

Moore appears to have been something of an enigmatic figure and there is comparatively little about him in standard reference books. There even seems to be some confusion over his initials; he is either J.N.H., N.H., or N.J.H., depending on which source is consulted. Apparently, the H stood for Hope. He had a long Bristol career, making 215 appearances from 1901 to 1910, and was clearly a talented place kicker. His club tally of 150 points was made up of 14 tries, 40 conversions, 8 penalties and a drop goal. Somerset handbooks state that he played for Bath at some stage, but again this is not confirmed in other sources. His county career is equally confusing as he represented both Gloucestershire and Somerset.

What is in no doubt is that he had the privilege of playing twice against the famous 1905 All Blacks. Bristol played this seminal team at the County Ground, losing 41-0, and Moore met up with the tourists again when Somerset played them at Jarvis's Field in Taunton. The score on this occasion was 23-0. Overturned wagons were used as a makeshift grandstand at this game. He also played for the combined Bristol and Clifton team against the 1908 Australian tourists. Again Moore finished on the losing side, this time 11-3. It is unfortunate that nothing else is known about Norman Moore as he was certainly one of Bristol's key players during the first decade of the twentieth century.

Alan Morley

Wing

Born: 25 June 1950

Career: 1969-86

Appearances: 519 games

Representative Honours: Gloucestershire, Public School Wanderers, Barbarians, England & Wales XV, England, British Lions

Tries: 384

Conversions: 4

Drop Goals: 1

Points: 1,516

Alan Morley was the most prolific try-scorer the sport of rugby union has seen. The world record try-scorer, he took great pride in his Bristol career and remains the holder of several club records.

A pupil at Colston's School, Morley was 'discovered' by David Rollitt, his maths and rugby teacher and Bristol number 8. Rollitt provided great encouragement and when Bristol held a mid-season trial match in 1968, Rollitt ensured Morley's name was put forward. He had a particularly successful game, scored a try and was invited to join Bristol.

Although still at school, he played for Bristol United against Abercarn at Christmas 1968 and made his First XV debut against Weston at the end of the season. He had no affiliation with a Combination club, but later played a handful of games for Old Colstonians.

Bristol had an embarrassment of riches on the wing, but Morley had talents that couldn't be ignored. Initially a centre, coach Peter Colston moved him closer to the touchline, explaining 'you don't like passing'! Whether by accident or design it was a seminal moment. Bristol suddenly had the most extraordinary try-scoring wing.

Morley possessed great anticipation, judgement and vision, although these qualities were only part of the story. Although not the fastest runner in the side, he could still swerve at top speed, had good hands and possessed the physique and power to hand off opponents. Crucially, he had the extraordinary footballing skills to make the most of even the merest of chances.

In the early part of his career, he was watched by the Welsh selectors. Qualifying for Wales through his Welsh mother, Morley opted for England before Welsh advances went too far. He was selected for England's tour to South Africa in 1972, scored a couple of tries in provincial matches and was then chosen for the international in Johannesburg. He received a telegram from Rees Stephens, chairman of Welsh Selectors: 'Heartiest congratulations. Good luck on Saturday from one Welshman to another.'

Morley scored the only try in a remarkable 18-9 victory. He played against New Zealand, Wales and Ireland the following year, but was not selected again until recalled to play Scotland in 1975, when he scored England's only try. He toured Australia that summer and played in both internationals. The second test, the 'Battle of Ballymore', was Morley's last international. Coincidentally, it was also the final England appearance of his mentor, Rollitt. Morley won a mere 7 caps for England.

He scored a record 4 tries for England against Western Australia on the 1975 tour, and he represented England and Wales against Scotland and Ireland in 1975 as part of the IRFU Centenary celebrations. The previous year he replaced Clive Rees on the British Lions tour in South Africa, and but for injury on the penultimate Saturday, might have played in the final test match.

He toured Italy with the Public School Wanderers in 1971 and was a member of their party which toured Zimbabwe in 1980, scoring 5 tries in one match against the hosts. He played for the Barbarians and represented Gloucestershire on 73 occasions, including several as captain.

There were many highlights in Morley's Bristol career. He scored 6 tries against Cheltenham in 1973 and crossed for 43 tries in the 1983/84 season, narrowly missing Mike Ellery's season's record of 44. Many of his most memorable Bristol tries were in the Cup, perhaps his most important being the match-winning score at the death against Plymouth Albion in 1974.

He played in the 1973, 1983 and 1984 cup finals, experiencing the joys of triumph and the despair of defeat. He was the only Bristol player to play in all these finals. Morley was vice-captain from 1978 to 1980, and again from 1982 to 1985. In between he captained Bristol, and although injured during the 1980/81 season, he top-scored with 21 tries. He was also voted Player of the Year, an award he won twice.

His last game for Bristol was against Eastern Ontario in June 1986. He had found his last season tough and was concerned he might keep younger players out of the side so he decided to retire. By then he had played 519 games for Bristol and crossed for 384 tries. These are Bristol career records which are unlikely to be beaten. He did pull on the Bristol United jersey twice in the 1988/89 season to help out and, inevitably, scored two tries. The following season he turned out twice for the Bristol 'A' side, a third XV

which functioned for a few seasons, and crossed for 4 more tries.

Morley was awarded the MBE for services to rugby in 1985 and was made an honorary vice-president of the club when he retired. He later helped Bob Hesford coach Bristol and then became Clifton coach. He also coached Bristol's wings on a personal basis in the late 1990s. He scored a world record 479 tries in first-class rugby. In both local and global terms, Alan Morley was truly a great player.

Ronnie Morris

Outside half

Born: 13 June 1913

Died: February 1983

Career: 1934-47

Appearances: 105 games

Representative Honours: Welsh Schools, Glamorgan, Gloucestershire, Wales

Tries: 18

Conversions: 4

Penalties: 2

Drop Goals: 28

Points: 180

Carmarthen-born Ronnie Morris played for Swansea when he was just seventeen and still a pupil at Queen Elizabeth's Grammar School. Originally a soccer player, when he converted to rugby he won his school cap and appeared for Welsh Schools against France. He captained South Wales Public Schools and was a regular in the Swansea side, usually at outside half, for 4 seasons. During this time he turned down an offer to play rugby league. When Cardiff scrum-half, Maurice Turnbull, withdrew from the Welsh team to play Scotland at Swansea in 1933, the selectors asked Turnbull's half-back partner, Harry Bowcott, to stand down so they could play Morris with his club partner, Bryn Evans. Unfortunately, Wales lost this game 11-3, and Morris did not retain his place.

Morris came to Bristol in 1934, his arrival coinciding with the retirement of centre Don Burland. Jimmy Barrington was Bristol's fly-half, so Morris played many games at centre, forming an excellent understanding with winger Harry Sherman. Later he shared the stand-off duties with Barrington, and, when injury forced Barrington's retirement, Morris made the position his own, developing a fine partnership with scrum-half Percy Redwood. He was Bristol's vice captain in 1937/38.

The Bristol *Jubilee Book* pays tribute to Morris's speed off the mark, his eye for a gap and his scoring of drop goals. Ironically, his most important drop goal was probably not a goal at all. When Gloucestershire played Kent in the 1937 county semi-final, the referee credited Morris with a successful drop goal when it was apparent to many that the ball had not passed between the posts. The Kent team lined up for a dropout and Morris told the referee that he thought he'd missed. The referee however insisted that the score should stand, Kent accepted the decision gracefully, and Gloucestershire won 7-5. Morris captained the county in the final, partnering Redwood in a 5-0 victory over East Midlands. He scored a try, but admitted that he was dazed at the time following a tackle and didn't really know what he was doing!

Morris was recalled by Wales to play Scotland at Swansea in 1937, becoming the first Bristol player to win a Welsh cap from the club. Wales lost 13-6. Morris, who also played for London Welsh, Crawshay's and Glamorgan, appeared for Bristol Supporters Team during the Second World War, and played for a short while afterwards, captaining Bristol United in 1946/47. He served on the committee for many years and was made an honorary life member in 1964.

Charlie Murphy
Back Row

Born: 17 October 1912

Died: 14 June 1989

Career: 1932-47

Appearances: 212

Representative Honours: England Schools, The South, Gloucestershire

Tries: 41

Points: 123

Charlie 'Spud' Murphy, a much-loved rugby character, was one of Bristol's best forwards of the 1930s and became one of a select band of players who appeared either side of the Second World War. A wing forward and a ferocious tackler, he played rugby at North Street School and when this school closed he moved to Castle Green School. His excellent record in schools rugby included games for Bristol Schools, the West XV and England Schools. He was selected for England as a hooker because he refused to stay onside as a wing forward! When he left school he joined St Mary's Old Boys.

Murphy made his Bristol United debut at Wiveliscombe in 1930/31, but had to wait two seasons for first-team action, eventually playing in a 7-5 victory at Oxford University in 1933. This was the first of four games for Murphy during the season, but the following year he really established himself. In a season of personal achievement he won his first-team cap, appeared in a county final for Gloucestershire and played for The South against The North in what was a revival of a traditional England trial match. He was outstanding for the county in the semi-final victory over Hampshire at Boscombe and this performance secured his place in the South side. For Bristol, he formed a powerful and speedy back-row combination with Arthur Payne and Bill Woodward.

Murphy remained in the Gloucestershire team for the rest of the decade. His 1934 final appearance ended in disappointment as East Midlands won 10-0, but three years later he was in the winning side against the same opposition in a final played at Bristol. He was awarded his Bristol blazer in 1935 and was leading appearance maker two years later. In 1937/38 he scored 11 tries, and he was named vice-captain for the ill-fated 1939/40 season which was abandoned when war broke out.

The war almost certainly robbed him of international honours. Murphy was a sergeant-major in the Army Physical Training Corps during the war, playing when he could for the Bristol Supporters Team, and guesting once for Newport. He was appointed vice-captain again in 1945 and starred for the Combined Gloucestershire and Somerset XV against the Kiwis. Despite retiring at the end of 1945/46, he made a final appearance against Cardiff the following season. He wrote regularly for the local press and as groundsman at St Brendan's College was responsible for laying out their rugby pitches. In later years he served as treasurer of the Bristol Old Players' Society and was made an honorary vice president by Bristol.

Born: May 1886

Died: 9 July 1967

Career: 1905-11

Appearances: 123 games

Representative Honours: British Isles, England, Barbarians, Gloucestershire

Tries: 65

Drop Goals: 2

Points: 203

Maurice Neale is one of a select group of players to have played international rugby for the British Isles before playing for his country. Possessing blistering speed off the mark, he was a highly prolific try-scorer.

Born in Thornbury the son of a Gloucestershire agriculturist, Neale lived on the Berkeley Estate. He was brought up on country sports and was a keen hunter. He was educated at Sir Thomas Riche's School, Gloucester and Prospect House, Dursley. A good athlete, he won boxing, cricket and 'jumping' honours as a seventeen year old.

Neale joined Bristol from the Eversley club as a centre, although Bristol utilised his pace predominantly on the wing. He made his debut against Bath in April 1905. For the next three seasons, Neale was Bristol's top try-scorer. He was an exceptional tackler, had the ability to kick the ball accurately with either foot and was an expert cross-kicker, qualities which, coupled with his pace, made Neale a complete footballer.

He played for the combined Bristol and

Clifton team against Australia in 1908 but badly injured his knee, missing the rest of the season and most of the following one. However, he returned towards the end of the 1909/10 season, showed good form for Bristol and Gloucestershire and was selected to tour South Africa with the British Isles team.

His selection was a surprise as he had not even appeared in an international trial or played much recent rugby. However, the selection proved to be inspired. He was ideally suited to the hard grounds and he played in all 3 tests, scored the winning try in the second international and ended the tour as top try-scorer, with 10. Three of this haul were obtained against Border, when Neale became only the second player to score a hat-trick in a British Isles jersey. He returned from tour a hero but failed to make the England side, although he was a travelling reserve during the 1911 international championship.

The following season he was Bristol captain but resigned the position after a heavy defeat by Newport in September, and subsequently joined Blackheath. He offered to appear in Bristol's Christmas matches but the furious committee would have none of it. He remained in London and eventually won his only cap against France, in 1912, as a centre. Maurice Neale, whose nephew Billy Neale was a popular Gloucestershire cricketer, returned to Bristol later in life and died in the city in 1967.

Derek Neate
Second row

Born: 2 July 1935

Career: 1952-72

Appearances: 393 games

Representative Honours: Gloucestershire, Western Counties, RAF, Combined Services, England trial

Tries: 73

Drop Goals: 1

Points: 222

Derek Neate, a second row or number eight who captained Bristol in two separate spells, had an incredible record of service. He made his Bristol United debut in 1952 and was still being called upon for occasional United games in the mid-1970s, playing his last game in 1977. Renowned for his lineout skills, powerful running and long passes, he was one of a crop of talented forwards who flourished during John Blake's open rugby era and he was unfortunate not to win an England cap.

Neate, who was educated at Portway School and Bristol Technical School, was originally a soccer player, but was converted to rugby by former Welsh international Les Williams. Neate was a scrum-half at Portway, a centre for Avonmouth Juniors and then a forward for Bristol Boys. He was spotted playing for Avonmouth Old Boys and invited for a Bristol trial. In his first season he played 21 United games and made his first-team debut in January 1953 against Harlequins. He was in and out of the first team for the next two seasons and was a member of the Bristol squad which appeared as a guest side in the first Snelling Sevens at Newport in 1954.

By 1955/56, Derek Neate was a regular first-team player. He appeared in 36 games during the season, the most by a forward, and unusually was awarded both his cap and his blazer. He was then called up for national service, so the RAF had first call on him for

the next two seasons. Fortunately he was stationed locally at Locking and Puckle-church and could turn out for Bristol when he was free. He played in 4 inter-service games for the RAF and in 1958 was a member of the side which won the inter-services championship by defeating the Royal Navy and drawing with the Army. He also appeared for the Combined Services, and in 1956/57 played in his first England trial as part of the Whites team which beat the Colours 20-0 at Bristol. Neate was unfortunate that his playing career coincided with those of such England line-out greats as John Currie and David Marques but even so he appeared in two more trials and was a travelling reserve for England on several occasions.

Neate returned to Bristol in 1958/59 after his spell in the RAF and was a regular in the first team for most of the next decade. He was Blake's vice-captain in 1960/61, playing in 43 of Bristol's 46 games and scoring 12 tries. He was appointed captain for the following season, during which he played 38 times. He continued as skipper for the 75th Anniversary season, a season badly disrupted by the severe winter, and was praised in the club's annual report for his excellent captaincy and his support at social functions.

Derek Neate was a regular in the Gloucestershire team for many years, making 48 county appearances in all. The county reached the Championship final in 1959 and he was a member of the side which lost 14-9 to the then-mighty Warwickshire at Bristol. He played twice for Western Counties against touring sides, appearing in the 42-0 loss to South Africa at Gloucester in 1960 and in the 22-14 defeat against New Zealand at Bristol three years later.

In 1965/66 Neate was invited to captain Bristol for a second spell, a rare honour, and led the side to one of its finest records. 39 games were won and 8 lost out of 47 and Bristol were crowned unofficial English champions. The number of victories was a new record which has been equalled since but not bettered. Neate played in 36 games during this memorable season, but was less fortunate in 1966/67 when illness and injury spoiled his final year as captain. He was able to play in only sixteen games, but inspired his team to a new points record of 862. Once again the annual report was unstinting in its praise of his leadership and service.

Derek Neate's retirement from the captaincy brought his regular playing days to an end, but he continued to serve the club as a committee member, coach and selector. He remained very fit and was always ready to turn out for the club if required. He played his final two first-team games in 1972 when Bristol were decimated by county calls, making his last appearance in a 28-3 victory at Weston-Super-Mare. His closing minutes in a first-team jersey were painful ones as he had to leave the field with a cut head following an accidental clash with team-mate Pete Sams. Even then, Bristol had not seen the last of his playing talents. He played 11 more United games over the next 4 seasons. When Alan Morley was injured in a United game at Cwmbran on New Year's Day 1977 he was replaced by Neate, who was then United coach, and who had tossed a coin with team secretary, Alan Ramsey, for the privilege of playing. Thus one of the club's greatest forwards appeared in a Bristol shirt 25 years after his first match.

Tony Nicholls
Outside half

Born: 24 October 1942

Career: 1966-75

Appearances: 311 games

Representative Honours: Sussex, Gloucestershire, South & South West, England trial

Tries: 44

Conversions: 102

Penalties: 97

Drop Goals: 43

Points: 77

Outside half Tony Nicholls was one of the club's greatest captains. He took over in 1971/72 and led Bristol to its best-ever record of 39 wins and 3 draws from 49 matches. Bristol scored 1,000 points in a season for the first time and were unofficial English/Welsh and English champions. Nicholls himself played in every game.

Tony Nicholls was educated at Hampton Grammar School and played for Southeast Schools. He attended Bristol University and Loughborough Colleges and played for Sussex Martlets, Haywards Heath and Rosslyn Park before coming to teach in Bristol, at Portway Comprehensive, Churchill, and latterly at Cotham Grammar. His Bristol debut was at centre against Gloucester in September 1966. He dropped a goal in the opening minutes of Bristol's 15-3 win, the first of his club career record of 43 and, again at centre, scored 16 points against London Irish the following week. Thereafter he settled at outside half and played 30 games in his first season, appearing in an England trial at Brighton. He also played in a friendly for Gloucestershire against Monmouthshire, having previously played 8 times for Sussex, but there was some doubt about his Gloucestershire eligibility and he was not selected again.

Nicholls partnered Bill Redwood in the final England trial in 1967/68, and was Bristol's leading scorer in the following two seasons, scoring a personal best of 171 in 1968/69. He was vice-captain to Dave Rollitt for two seasons and then commenced his three-year stint of leadership. Bristol responded superbly to his calm yet inspirational captaincy and following the glories of his first year in charge he led the club to the 1973 cup final. Bristol were trailing at half time in the semi-final at London Welsh, but Nicholls, goaded by a foolishly premature Tannoy announcement about tickets for the final, rallied his side to a superb second-half recovery and an 18-15 win.

Nicholls was invited to be captain for a third year and had the satisfaction of winning another unofficial English title with Bristol, as well as appearing with nine club colleagues in the South and South West team which defeated Australia at Bath. During his captaincy Bristol defeated each side they played at least once with the exception of Bedford who beat Bristol twice and drew in 1973/74. Nicholls, who was chaired from the field after his final game as captain, played 19 matches in the following season before bowing out of top rugby. He then played for Old Bristolians, serving for a while as a Bristol selector, a duty he admitted to find harder than playing. He currently coaches at Bristol Cathedral School.

Jimmy Oates
Full-back

Born: Unknown

Died: 1955/56

Career: 1896-1910

Appearances: 299 games

Representative Honours: Gloucestershire

Tries: 1*

Conversions: 85*

Penalties: 6*

Drop Goals: 3*

Points: 203*

* scoring details from 1900-10 only

'No words can indicate what he has done for the club ever since he first joined it; no one has achieved more valuable out of sight work, often of the most exacting kind.'

Thus the Bristol *Jubilee Book* summed up the contribution of Jimmy Oates, who served the club as a player and administrator for over fifty years. A full-back, he received his first-team cap in 1896/97, was vice-captain from 1902 to 1904 and captained Bristol in the 1905/06 season. He was Bristol's leading appearance maker for many years, his total of 299 games eventually being beaten by Fred Coventry in the 1920s, and he was also a prolific points scorer.

Jimmy Oates made 20 appearances for Gloucestershire. He was Bristol's full-back when the club defeated Cardiff for the first time, and his season of captaincy coincided with the visit of the first All Blacks. Their game with Bristol was Oates's second match as captain, but he was out of action for much of the season through injury and retired at the

end of it. He was immediately made an honorary life member.

Oates was assistant secretary from 1907 to 1909 and then joint secretary with various people from 1910 to 1914, a period when as many as three shared the job. He stepped in at short notice to act as secretary for the A XV (as Bristol's Second XV was then called) in 1924/25 and in 1926/27, more than 20 years after the end of his playing career, he actually made one appearance for the A XV, even managing to kick a conversion. He was a major figure in the Old Players' Society, acting as honorary secretary, and enjoyed attending reunions with fellow players. At one such gathering in 1938 he summed up his love for the club in these words: 'I have never lost my interest in the club – in fact it is keener than ever.'

Oates remained on the committee after the Second World War, celebrating 50 years of service to Bristol in 1945/46 and finally retiring from committee work in 1947. He was made president of the Old Players' Society in 1955, but by then he was in poor health and he died during the 1955/56 season. Few have matched his record of service to the club he loved.

Born: 21 January 1909

Died: 6 June 1968

Career: 1931-38

Appearances: 162 games

Representative Honours: Gloucestershire, England

Tries: 5

Points: 15

Arthur Payne achieved the unusual distinction of gaining an England cap without featuring in a trial game. When England faced Wales at Twickenham on 19 January 1935 it was the first time since 1931, a total of 11 games, that Bristol had no representative in the team. Following a rather dull 3-3 draw, England made three changes for the following game and Payne was brought into the middle of the back row in place of Dudley Kemp of Blackheath, who thus became a 'one-cap wonder'. Payne's debut saw England defeat Ireland 14-3 at Twickenham and he retained his place for the next game, a 10-7 loss to Scotland at Murrayfield. That was the end of England's season – France were not played at that time owing to suspicions of professionalism – and it was also the end of Arthur Payne's international career. Despite showing good form in the following season, he was injured at the wrong time and was unable to add to his caps.

A member of the long-established Bristol Combination team Dings Crusaders, where his brother, Frederick, was captain, Arthur Payne made his Bristol debut against Royal Naval Engineering College in October 1931 and was awarded his first-team cap at the end of the season. He was Bristol's leading appear-ance maker in 1932/33 and won his blazer the following year, during which he also made his Gloucestershire debut. He became renowned for his line-out expertise, his work rate in open play and his tactical kicking. In partnership with Charlie Murphy and Bill Woodward he formed a formidable back-row unit, and the three played together many times for Bristol. The club's *Jubilee Book* referred to them as a 'deadly trio'.

Payne, who later moved to the second row, played 15 times for Gloucestershire and appeared in the 1934 County Championship final in which the county lost to East Midlands. His final game for Bristol was at Cardiff in 1937, after which he returned to Dings, whom he captained. He was heavily involved with the Boys Clubs both locally and nationally and worked as an aircraft engineer at Filton. Arthur Payne was a noted club cricketer and wrote for Bristol's local sports papers.

Alan Pearn
Scrum-half

Born: 25 June 1948

Career: 1970-79

Appearances: 286 games

Representative Honours: Devon, South West Counties, South & South West, Devon & Cornwall

Tries: 67

Conversions: 362

Penalties: 342

Drop Goals: 12

Points: 2,047

Alan Pearn was one of Bristol's most influential players. He was an imperious goal kicker, and a scrum-half with a pass the length, speed and accuracy of which has rarely been seen at the Memorial Ground before or since.

Pearn joined Bristol in 1970 having qualified as a teacher at St Luke's College, Exeter. As a youngster at Okehampton Grammar School he wavered between soccer and rugby. He played rugby for the school on Saturday morning, captaining the side, and soccer for Lewdown Rovers in the afternoon. He had a trial for Plymouth Argyle but it was the emphasis on rugby at St Luke's which influenced the direction of his sporting career.

Whilst at St Luke's, Pearn played for South West Counties against South Africa where his opponent was Dawie de Villiers. He was instrumental in the successes of the student side, which was then a very strong team, and played for Plymouth Albion when home from college.

Pearn began his teaching career in Midsomer Norton, and joined Bristol. His debut was at Cross Keys in the first match of the 1970/71 season. He played in 33 of Bristol's games and scored 175 points, including 7 tries. Although he was top points-scorer, there were significant contributions from vice-captain Tony Nicholls and Bruce Thompson.

He formed a potent half-back partnership with Nicholls with whom he shared an almost telepathic understanding. The quiet Nicholls benefited greatly from Pearn's remarkable pass. A master of the reverse pass, Pearn could deliver the ball with pinpoint accuracy to colleagues over half the width of the pitch away. It offered a new dimension to Bristol's play, and under coach Peter Colston the team blossomed. In 1971/72, the club won 39 of its 49 games, only losing 7 matches all season. Bristol amassed 1,145 points and scored 177 tries, 16 by Pearn.

A courageous and intelligent player, it was goal-kicking which drew Pearn's name to the attention of the public. During 1971/72 he shattered Gordon Cripps's points record with 429, which he extended to 452 the following season. He kicked a record 10 conversions against Plymouth Albion, in March 1972, and scored 26 points, also then a record, against Bègles in September 1972. His haul was made up of 1 try, 2 conversions, 5 penalties and 1 dropped goal.

A regular Devon player for many years, he also played for Devon and Cornwall against Fiji in 1970, South and South West against the RFU President's XV in the RFU Centenary tour of 1971, South West Counties against New Zealand in 1973, and scored 11 points in the South and South West's 15-14 victory over Australia later that year.

A statistician's dream, in the 1972/73 season Pearn scored 557 points in all his rugby, being the only British player to pass 500 points, and the first to 100, 200, 300 and 400 points. He scored 17 tries in all, plus 69 conversions, 109 penalties and 8 dropped goals. He scored all 24 points for Devon against Romania and all 15 for Bristol in the 1973 cup final against Coventry. He had a terrific game for Bristol at Kingsholm in September 1972 when Bristol's 13-9 win took Gloucester's unbeaten ground record.

Yet all this was largely ignored elsewhere. Pearn was chosen for the England squad during the 1971 Five Nations and was a bench replacement for the match against Scotland. Although he didn't play, the producers of the match programme thought he might – they printed his photograph believing it to be that of Alan Cowman, the outside half!

He played in a regional trial for England but was otherwise ignored. Whilst he continued to pass with length and accuracy, kick goals and score tries he was overlooked whilst others of inferior ability were capped in England teams. A largely unrecognised talent, Pearn was never capped by England. What was England's loss, and indeed Pearn's, was Bristol's gain. During the 1970s he wore the 'G' shirt with pride and was a dominant figure throughout the decade.

As Richard Harding's career developed at Bristol so Pearn's began to wind down. Thus one superb scrum-half was replaced by another, although quite different in style. Pearn's last game for Bristol was against Clifton in March 1979. He played a couple of games for Bristol United the following season before leaving the club and playing occasional social rugby for Thornbury.

Alan Pearn's total of 2,047 points remained Bristol's career record until Mark Tainton broke it in 1997. However, the 452 points scored in 1972/73 remains the club's record for a season.

A PE teacher at the Castle School in Thornbury, he worked with former Bristol player Roy Dash. He taught at the school for twenty-nine years until taking early retirement in 2002.

The Pearn name continues in top sport. Alan Pearn's son Mark is an international hockey player, having played for Great Britain in the 2000 Olympics and England in the 2002 Commonwealth Games.

Agustín Pichot
Scrum-half

Born: 22 August 1974

Career: 1999-2002

Appearances: 74 games

Representative Honours: Argentina U19, Argentina U21, Barbarians, Argentina

Tries: 19

Conversions: 1

Drop Goals: 1

Points: 100

Agustín Pichot is one of the most charismatic players to have played for Bristol. An Argentinean, he is his country's most famous rugby player of recent times and a true icon for the sport throughout the world.

Born in Buenos Aires, he was educated at St John the Baptist School and Buenos Aires University. His father played rugby for Club Atlético San Isidro, as did his older brother Enrique. Young Agustín greatly admired his brother and followed his career intently, eventually playing for San Isidro himself. Pichot was a football fan in a soccer-mad country, but the family's sport was rugby so he followed tradition and pursued a career in the game, much to the delight of his enthusiastic father and grandfather.

An accomplished sevens player, Pichot was capped by Argentina at Under-19 and Under-21 levels. He made a try-scoring debut for the Pumas against Australia in 1995, and was in the Argentina squad for the 1995 World Cup, although he didn't play. He then suffered a serious knee injury which prevented him from playing for most of 1996 and 1997.

Pichot joined Richmond in 1997 and played for them in the premier division for two seasons until they collapsed financially in

1999. Signed by Bristol in the close season, he played in the Argentina side that reached the quarter-finals of the 1999 World Cup and made his club debut against Northampton immediately after the tournament. He made an instant impression and he helped ensure that Bristol's first season back in the top division was successful. An all-action dynamo, the constantly moving Pichot caused headaches for countless defences with his darts around the fringes from set piece and second phase play, and his quickly taken penalties were constant threats.

A distinctive figure, Pichot was Bristol captain for the 2000/01 season. He captained Bristol and scored the only try in their first league victory over Bath in December 2000, and he was instrumental in bringing compatriot Felipe Contepomi to the club, forming a fine half-back partnership with him.

An unpredictable player possessing flair and vision, he has played for the Barbarians on 7 occasions, and scored a magnificent try against South Africa in 2002. Pichot regularly captains Argentina and has scored 10 tries for his country in over 40 international matches.

His grandfather was a contemporary of Salvador Dalí, and Pichot shares his ancestor's interest in surrealist art. 1999 Argentine Sportsman of the Year, Agustín Pichot remains a high-profile Bristol player and one upon whom the club can rely to secure future successes.

Reg Pickles
Centre

Born: 11 December 1895

Died: November 1978

Career: 1912-27

Appearances: 244 games

Representative Honours: Gloucestershire, Mother Country, England

Tries: 70

Conversions: 94

Penalties: 32

Drop Goals: 4

Points: 510

Reg Pickles was Bristol's first captain after the First World War and he had the honour of leading his side to a 19-3 victory over Cardiff on the occasion of the first-ever game at the Memorial Ground. Later that season he received his two England caps, both as a full-back, despite the fact that he played most of his club games at centre. His England debut was in the 12-3 win against Ireland in Dublin, and he retained his place for the next match, a fortunate 11-11 draw with France at Twickenham. This was not a happy game for Pickles. His defensive fumble led to one of the French tries and he was not selected for the final international of the season against Scotland.

Pickles played for Bristol either side of the First World War. His talent was nurtured at Bristol Grammar School, where he captained the First XV, and he received his Bristol cap at the end of the 1913/14 season. During this season he played in Bristol's unexpected 22-17 victory at Newport. He had a distinguished war record, serving in the Royal Engineers and winning the Military Cross. He was wounded at Arras. After the war he played for the interim Bristol United side which operated during the 1918/19 season and appeared in the King's Cup inter-services

tournament, representing the Mother Country against Canada, New Zealand and South Africa. The Bristol club was relaunched in 1919 and Pickles was captain for the first game, a 21-6 victory over Bridgwater. He was skipper for three seasons in all.

Reg Pickles frequently partnered Len Corbett in the centre for Bristol and the two were often paired together for Gloucestershire. The early 1920s were vintage years for the county and a hat-trick of championship titles was won. Pickles appeared in all 3 finals, once as a centre and twice as full-back. He captained the county in the 1921 final, a 31-4 victory over Leicestershire at Gloucester. He also played in the losing final of 1925, and, again with Corbett, played in the county side which lost only 6-0 to the invincible Second All Blacks. In all, the powerful, versatile Pickles played 28 county matches. He is remembered as one of Bristol's best captains, leading a free-scoring side at an important time in the club's history.

Ken Plummer

Wing

Born: 17 January 1947

Career: 1968-78

Appearances: 269 games

Representative Honours: Cornwall, South West Counties, Devon & Cornwall XV, Barbarians, England

Tries: 139

Drop Goals: 1

Points: 498

Ken Plummer was one of the fastest wings to have played for Bristol. An entertaining player, he was a key member of the Bristol side for many years and a popular captain.

He was educated at Penryn County Secondary School and first played for the Penryn club as a sixteen year old. Possessing blistering pace, he held junior and senior Cornish sprinting titles at the same time. He made his Cornwall debut aged seventeen and went on to play 52 games for the county. He toured with the Barbarians at Easter 1968 whilst a Penryn player.

Plummer moved from Penryn's Memorial Ground to Bristol's in the summer of 1968, and he made his debut in the first match of the 1968/69 season, against Northern on a short tour of the north east. He formed an effective strike partnership with fellow wing Mike Collins, and in his first season top-scored with 21 tries from his 31 games for the club.

He made his England debut against Wales in 1969 in a match that heralded the start of the second golden era of Welsh rugby. An unhappy time was had by all in white, and

Plummer had to wait until 1976 to earn further caps. He played against Scotland when Alan Morley dropped out and held his place for the rest of the season. He won 4 international caps in all.

A groin strain precluded Plummer from playing in the 1973 Cup final, unquestionably the biggest disappointment of his career. However, he recovered sufficiently to assist Newport on their tour to South Africa a few weeks later.

He represented South West Counties against Australia in 1967 (aged nineteen), and played in games against South Africa, Fiji, New Zealand (scoring a try in 1973) and for Devon & Cornwall against Australia in 1975. Plummer became Bristol's captain in 1976/77 and was skipper again the following season. During the 1977/78 season he suffered a dislocated shoulder and when he injured it again against Gloucester in February 1978 he decided to retire from playing. He was elected to the Bristol committee and served for a few seasons. He coached Keynsham for two seasons, playing occasionally for them, before stepping down to coach Keynsham Youth.

A motor mechanic, Plummer worked for Bryan Brothers. He moved into vehicle sales and pursued a successful career with the company which saw him become group managing director. When Ken Plummer retired from Bryan Brothers he returned to Cornwall where he is now chairman of his old club, Penryn.

Peter Polledri
Flanker

Born: 10 June 1957

Career: 1975-90

Appearances: 466 games

Representative Honours: England Schools U19, England Students, British Universities, England U23, Gloucestershire

Tries: 84

Points: 366

Peter Polledri was one of the most creative and underrated of all Bristol players. One third of the back row that won the cup in 1983, he came close to playing rugby for Italy.

Born in Bristol of Italian parents, Polledri began playing rugby aged eight at St Brendan's, where he later played for the college as a scrum-half. He was coached and guided by the influential Elwyn Price, and was also a good cricketer. He moved into the back row and was capped by England Schools Under-19s. Polledri played for Bristol Colts and after serving his apprenticeship was promoted to the Bristol side. He made his debut against Saracens in October 1975.

As a youngster, he was an admirer of Dave Rollitt, and the Yorkshireman was still a Bristol player when Polledri joined the First XV squad. Rollitt had a considerable influence on his career.

Polledri was a great footballer. The ball-handling skills he had used so successfully as a teenage scrum-half gave him an added dimension. Small, but compact and very strong, he fitted in perfectly with Mike Rafter and Bob Hesford during the 1980s. Equally at home foraging on the floor or supporting a three-quarter move, Polledri was remarkably fit. His versatility was perfectly illustrated when he deputised for the injured Richard Harding against West Hartlepool on the way to the 1983 cup final. Polledri's contribution was significant and helped secure a narrow but famous victory.

Polledri played for Gloucestershire, making his debut for the county in the 62-10 victory over Japan in 1976. He represented England Students, and British Universities when at UWIST in Cardiff. He played regularly for England Under-23s and later captained them. Despite this, England wanted taller back-row forwards and although Rafter had broken into the national side, Polledri was not required.

However, whilst on tour in the mid-1980s, Polledri played for an Italian selection. He was encouraged to move to Italy and play there for a season with great prospects of selection for Italy. Sorely tempted, Polledri turned down the opportunity as he had just opened a business in Bristol and felt that it had to take priority.

Polledri succeeded Rafter as Bristol captain and served for two seasons, although he suffered with injuries during his tenure. He was Bristol United captain from 1988 to 1990 after which he left and joined Clifton. He later coached them and played into his early forties with Clifton Rats, the veterans team. Peter Polledri is now the head coach at St Mary's Old Boys.

Nigel Pomphrey

Lock/back row

Born: 11 January 1957

Career: 1976-88

Appearances: 364 games

Representative Honours: Gloucestershire, Barbarians, England U23, England B, England XV

Tries: 130

Points: 520

Nigel Pomphrey was one of the most athletic forwards to have played for Bristol. Captain in the centenary year, he selflessly put the club before his personal rugby career and consequently missed out on the chance of an international cap.

Educated at St Brendan's College, Pomphrey was initially guided by the inspirational Elwyn Price, and played number 8. A multi-talented sportsman, he played rugby for Bristol Colts and Gloucestershire schools at Under-16 level and was a shot-put and discus thrower with Westbury Harriers. He won a silver medal in the discus in AAA Junior championships and was at one time a South West junior weightlifting champion.

Pomphrey chose to play rugby in preference to other sports, despite not coming from a rugby family. He played for Bristol United during school holidays from the age of sixteen and was a replacement for the First XV when 17.

He made his debut for Bristol in the cauldron of Kingsholm in September 1976. Chosen at lock, he had a memorable game, which Bristol won, and he joined many of his Gloucester opponents a few weeks later in the Gloucestershire side when still only eighteen years old.

Pomphrey was big, strong and mobile. He possessed remarkable pace and acceleration, had ball-handling skills more commonly associated with a centre, and was spring-heeled and agile. He was an admirer of Welsh lock Allan Martin. Pomphrey's Bristol career overlapped that of Dave Rollitt and Bristol's vastly experienced former captain guided and assisted him in the facts of first-class rugby life. It was clear Pomphrey was an exceptional talent and Rollitt was determined that talent should not be wasted. He had a considerable influence on the young forward.

Pomphrey was equally comfortable in the second row and back row. He was a regular first-team player in his first season, and he was selected for England B in his second. In the autumn of 1977 he sat on the replacements bench for an England XV against the USA, although he was not required to play. However, it was the 1978/79 season that really saw Pomphrey blossom. He scored 22 tries in his 34 games for Bristol, more than any other player that season and more than any other forward in a season before or since. At the end of the season he was chosen to tour the Far East with England, where he accompanied Rafter, Hignell and Doubleday.

Despite playing in the test matches against Japan, Fiji and Tonga, Pomphrey remained without full international honours as caps were not awarded. He had been chosen to tour as a lock but played predominantly at blind-side flank forward. He scored two tries in the match against Kyushu, and repeated the feat in the second international against Japan. He was a revelation. His mobility and power were never more clearly demonstrated than on those hard grounds.

England selector Budge Rogers advised him that if he played in Bristol's back row he would be capped. But with Messrs Baker, Rafter, Polledri and Hesford already battling it out for back-row places, competition was tough. A few matches in the United back row preceded a lengthy period at lock for the firsts. Bristol needed him in the second row. Loyalty came first, and despite later captaining England Under-23s, Pomphrey was never capped. It is clear that had he moved clubs it might have been different. He was courted by Newport, Gloucester and particularly Cardiff and had approaches from rugby league. But Pomphrey was a proud Bristolian and any such move was never an option.

Pomphrey was a regular player with Gloucestershire. His appearances for the Barbarians included the 1981 Hong Kong Sevens tournament. The Barbarians won the tournament, although Pomphrey missed the final with a pulled hamstring. In the blue and white of Bristol, Pomphrey was as committed as ever. He played in the 1983 Cup Final victory, and in the narrow defeat in the Cup Final the following year. He was honoured with the club captaincy for the 1986/87 and 1987/88 seasons, the latter being the club's centenary season. At the end of the centenary season he captained Bristol in the cup final.

The 1988 Cup Final defeat was his last game for Bristol. He had announced his intention to retire after the semi-final victory over Moseley. Although capable of carrying on playing, he didn't want to just fade away. He had no affiliation to a combination club and so decided to stop playing when his form was good and he could still command a place in the Bristol first XV. He was now able to devote time to his young family and his job as a director of the family engineering business. He was made an honorary vice-president and later served on the club committee.

Pomphrey still holds the club's career try-scoring record for a forward with 130, a record he took from Dave Rollitt. Unfortunate to play at a time when forwards pushed, shoved and merely won the ball, there is little doubt Nigel Pomphrey was a rugby player ahead of his time.

Nigel Pomphrey powers through the Harlequins defence, with winger John Lane in support.

Doug Pratten

Back row

Born: 12 October 1922

Died: 18 May 1997

Career: 1945-53

Appearances: 217 games

Representative Honours: Gloucestershire, Western Counties

Tries: 40

Conversions: 2

Penalties: 1

Points: 127

Doug Pratten appeared as a winger in his first season, but soon became an established member of Bristol's back row. He played rugby at St Brendan's College, attended Bristol University, and made his Bristol debut at Cardiff in December 1945, the first of seven appearances during the season. He gained his club cap at the end of 1946/47 and his blazer two years later.

Pratten played in 34 games during 1949/50 and was vice-captain to Denzil Golledge the following year. He was a regular Gloucestershire player and appeared in the 1949 final defeat against Lancashire. He also played for Stanley's XV against Oxford University and was carded for an England trial. He succeeded Golledge as captain in 1951/52, and although this was not a good year for Bristol, Pratten himself had an excellent season. He jointly topped Bristol's appearances with 34 games, and captained Gloucestershire. At the same time club colleague, Michael Corbett, captained Somerset, and it was Corbett who was selected to lead the Western Counties XV against South Africa at Bristol. Pratten played in the game and was involved in a crucial incident. With the South Africans leading 8-5, home winger Jack Gregory made a superb 80-yard break before handing what appeared to be a scoring pass to Pratten. Pratten duly touched down, but the referee judged that Gregory's pass had been forward and disallowed the score. The visitors went on to win 16-5, and many wondered what might have happened had Pratten's score stood.

Doug Pratten played another season for Bristol before going on to enjoy his rugby at Cheltenham, while continuing to train at the Memorial Ground. Before he left Bristol he was instrumental in gaining a greater say for the players in the selection of the club captain. This followed the decision of the committee to re-elect Jack Gregory as captain in 1953, despite the players' preference for Glyn Davies. Pratten's motion on behalf of the players at the club AGM was carried easily and their views carried much greater weight from then on.

Doug Pratten, an incredibly fit man, continued in active rugby for many years, latterly playing for Old Cothamians. He was turning out for the lower fifteens in his late fifties. He taught at Cotham Grammar School and wrote a history of the school. He continued his association with Bristol, serving as membership secretary and secretary of the Old Players' Society. His dedication to Bristol was rewarded in 1994 when he was made an honorary life member.

John Pullin

Hooker

Born: 1 November 1941

Career: 1961-78

Appearances: 296 games

Representative Honours: Gloucestershire, Barbarians, England, British Isles

Tries: 11

Points: 36

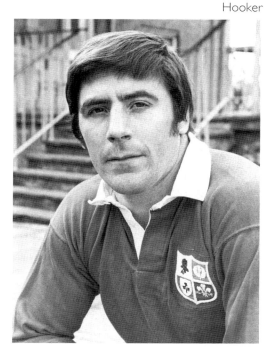

John Pullin was undoubtedly one of the greatest of all Bristol players, yet his finest achievements were in the jerseys of England and the British Lions.

Educated at Thornbury Grammar School and the Royal Agricultural College, Cirencester, he joined Bristol Saracens as a youngster, occasionally playing as a prop. After four seasons he attended a trial at the Memorial Ground and joined Bristol.

His debut was a baptism of fire. He played, as a twenty year old, in the Bristol scrum against Newport, in September 1961 where his opponent was Bryn Meredith, current Welsh and Lions hooker. He survived this experience, Bristol won, and he played the following 14 games.

Pullin had already worn the blue and white jersey for Bristol United when a Saracens player. He played 6 times for the United in both the 1959/60 and 1960/61 seasons.

John Thorne was Bristol's first-choice hooker, but Pullin established himself after Thorne's appearances for England in 1963. At one stage, both men played in the front row, with Thorne a very capable prop. The experienced David Hazell helped him develop technique, particularly scrummaging. He possessed impeccable striking skills – at a time when heels against the head were common Pullin almost always out-struck his opponent. He initially played when wings threw the ball into the line-out, a role he later had to master.

He was immensely strong, having the natural strength which comes of being a livestock farmer. Such was the power of his grip that his props regularly came off the field with bruises to their ribs where Pullin had bound so tightly. A quiet and conscientious man, Pullin was very fit through work on the family farm in the shadow of the Severn Bridge, and he supplemented his club training by running to Wales and back over the bridge.

In the autumn of 1965 Pullin was selected for Gloucestershire, and after featuring in three trials he played for England against Wales in 1966. His rapid arrival in the England team was followed by even quicker ejection, and it was to be two years before he won his second cap, again against Wales. However, Pullin had established himself in the England side on the 1967 summer tour to Canada.

In 1968 he toured South Africa with the British Lions. He was injured at the start of the tour, and was unavailable for the first test, but he recovered and played in the three remaining internationals. He also played in the defeat by Transvaal, which was considered physically harder than the tests. He fell foul of South African refereeing interpretations of the striking laws in the second test, and in the third test, he was knocked virtually unconscious by an off-the-ball punch.

England against the touring Springboks later that year. He toured South Africa again in 1972, this time as captain of England. Pullin believes this tour was successful because the selectors stayed at home. The tour culminated in victory over South Africa in Johannesburg.

Pullin led England to victory over New Zealand in Auckland the following summer, after an indifferent Five Nations campaign. He was joined on tour by his understudy at Bristol, John White. Remarkably, the international was the only game won by the tourists. He also captained England in Australia in 1975.

He continued as captain even though domestically England were far from successful. The political troubles in Ireland had precluded matches being played in Dublin in 1972, but after England's defeat there in 1973 Pullin produced one of rugby's greatest ever quotations: 'We may not be very good but at least we turn up!' Pullin eventually won 42 England caps, then a record, and captained England to victories over all the major nations except Ireland.

He played for the Barbarians on 19 occasions, most famously in the 1973 encounter with New Zealand. He was involved in the great try scored by Gareth Edwards, and played a prominent role in the 23-11 victory. Remarkably, Pullin played New Zealand in 7 international and equivalent matches of which only 2 were lost. He later became a Barbarian committeeman.

Pullin played in the 1973 Cup Final for Bristol, but not for long. He suffered a serious knee injury immediately after kick off and had to leave the field. As this was before replacements were permitted at club level Bristol continued with 14 men, but lost despite a courageous effort.

His last match for Bristol was at Gosforth in April 1978. Pullin then devoted himself to his family and business. He had worked on his farm as much as possible during his career, which accounts for only 296 appearances for Bristol in 17 seasons. There can rarely have been a player who enjoyed more success on the rugby field than John Pullin.

Pullin was a Lion again three years later on the much heralded tour of New Zealand. He played in all 4 tests, which saw the first Lions series win in New Zealand. He featured in the notorious games against Hawkes Bay, the Maoris and Canterbury, after which both his props returned home injured.

He toured South Africa with the Barbarians in 1969 and scored a try for

Reg Quick
Wing

Born: 11 April 1895

Died: 28 May 1978

Career: 1913-28

Appearances: 261 games

Representative Honours: Somerset, England trial

Tries: 190

Drop Goals: 1

Points: 574

Reg Quick was one of the most prolific try-scorers in the history of the Bristol club. His 33 tries in the 1920/21 season was a club record until Mike Ellery beat it over forty years later, and he scored a grand total of 190 in 261 appearances. Although he played his early games for the club in the centre it was as a left-winger that he achieved his remarkable try-scoring feats in the years immediately following the First World War. The characteristic feature of his play was a high-kicking run which made him extremely difficult to tackle, and he formed a superb understanding with centre Len Corbett as an integral part of an exciting three-quarter line.

Quick first played the game at St Mary Redcliffe School in 1908, captaining the school XV in the following year, when he and Corbett played in the Bristol Schools side. He sang in Redcliffe Church choir, and excelled at athletics, winning several gold medals as a sprinter in schools competitions. He trained by running on the cobbled streets around the school. After a brief flirtation with soccer, when he considered signing for Bristol City, he opted for rugby and joined Bristol in the last season before the First World War, winning his Second XV cap, and playing a few first-team games, including the last one of the pre-war era, a 14-3 defeat to Aberavon.

Reg Quick was an early recruit when war broke out, joining the 1st South Midland: Gloucestershire Brigade Royal Field Artillery.

He became a proficient horseman and served with distinction throughout the war as a signaller, winning the Italian Croix de Guerre for bravery and being recommended for a Military Medal for conspicuous gallantry repairing telephone lines and manning a visual station under heavy bombardment.

When the war finished, Quick became a member of the interim Bristol United team which operated during 1918/19, scoring 10 tries. The Bristol club was relaunched the following season and Quick played in the opening game, scoring a try in the victory over Bridgwater. By the end of that season he had scored 20 tries, won his first-team cap and been selected for Somerset. He set his club record in the next season, when perhaps his most important and spectacular score was a brilliant individual effort in a famous 13-6 defeat of Newport at Bristol City's Ashton Gate ground. The bulk of Bristol's home games at this time were played on a makeshift

Quick for many reasons. He became the first Bristol player to receive the newly introduced award of a blazer for playing 70 first-team games, and he was appointed captain of Somerset, a post he held until 1927. He also played for England against The North in a trial, the closest he got to the international honours he so richly deserved. He became Bristol captain in 1922/23, scored 32 tries again, and on 23 December in the game with Old Merchant Taylors, crossed for his 100th post-war try for the club. This was the season in which Somerset won the County Championship, defeating Leicestershire at Bridgwater, but Quick was unable to lead his side in the final as he was injured playing for Bristol against Bath on the previous Wednesday.

Reg Quick continued with what the annual report called his 'genial and happy' leadership of Bristol in 1923/24, enjoying the team's visit to France, where he scored a try in the 8-6 win against Cognac. In the following season he captained his county in the game against the New Zealand All Blacks, and scored a further 26 club tries. His form gradually declined as the decade progressed and he stepped down to captain Bristol's Second XV in 1927/28, although he still played for Somerset. This was Quick's final season as a Bristol player, but by no means the end of his association with the club. He joined the committee in 1929 and stayed there for the next thirty-two years, eventually acting as chairman from 1954 until his retirement in 1961. He also continued his links with Somerset and was county president from 1955 to 1961, as well as being an honorary member of the Rugby Football Union.

When Reg Quick retired as chairman in 1961 he ended an official association with the Bristol club which stretched back nearly fifty years. There was a special presentation to mark the occasion, and the following appeared in the annual report: 'We who have worked with him for so many years realise what a loss he will be to Rugby Football.' Reg Quick, besides being one of Bristol's very greatest players, was a dedicated worker for the club he loved.

ground at Radnor Road. The pitch had a pronounced dip in one corner and Quick scored tries there so regularly that it was christened 'Quick's Corner' by the club's supporters. When the Memorial Ground was opened in September 1921, Quick scored two of Bristol's tries in the 19-3 victory over Cardiff and was on 32 for the season and looking certain to beat his own record when an injury against Bradford on Easter Tuesday thwarted him.

The 1921/22 season was memorable for

Mike Rafter

Flanker

Born: 31 March 1952

Career: 1972-84

Appearances: 255 games

Representative Honours: England U19, England U23, Barbarians, Devon, Gloucestershire, England & Wales XV, England, Public School Wanderers

Tries: 30

Points: 120

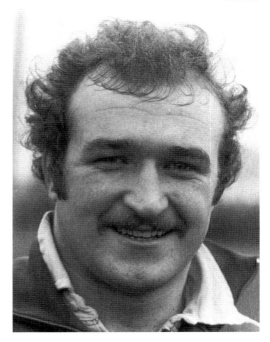

Mike Rafter was Bristol's captain for one of the most successful seasons in the club's history. An inspirational player, he was a rugby philosopher and visionary who was cruelly treated by national rugby selectors.

An all-action player, Rafter became a rugby player by chance. A football fanatic, he had a trial for Bristol City at the age of fourteen, but went to St Brendan's College where he was introduced to rugby and coached by Elwyn Price. It was Price who guided him from a position of occasional scrum-half in house rugby to college back row, to which he was ideally suited. He would regularly play rugby for the college on Saturday mornings and soccer for Hotwells in the afternoon. However, rugby was in his blood: his maternal grandmother was Sam Tucker's sister.

Fit, strong and with a rare creative eye, Rafter soon played rugby for Bristol Colts, where he first got the chance to play at the Memorial Ground. He also played for England Under-19s.

Rafter studied at St Luke's College, Exeter, and captained a strong side which included several future international players. He represented Devon whilst a student there and played for Bristol, Bristol United and occasionally Old Ashtonians when home from college. His Bristol debut was at Exeter in April 1973, but early in the 1973/74 season he captained the United and was First XV pack leader in a remarkable 13-12 win at Swansea. The young Rafter had already made an impact

and responded to the responsibility. He was man of the match.

Fast and pugnacious, Rafter was highly motivated. He always gave 100 per cent, irrespective of whom he played for. He was rarely more than a few feet from the ball and epitomised the support skills integral to the play of a wing forward. He was totally reliable and with Peter Polledri and Bob Hesford formed a back row on which the rest of the team was able to depend. When the ball went to ground, Rafter and co. were there to gather, protect and recycle. They were also a devastating attacking unit and worked hard on their unit skills. They perfected attacking moves and several, such as one called 'Pete's move', ripped the opposition apart. Even those who knew what was coming couldn't defend against it.

Capped at Under-23 level, Rafter played in a trial for England in 1976 before making his debut in a resounding 26-6 victory over Scotland in 1977. He toured the Far East in 1979 and was a member of England's 1980 Grand Slam squad. He played the last of his 17 internationals in Argentina on England's 1981 tour. Awarded man of the match in both

tests, he was mysteriously dropped upon his return for the youthful Peter Winterbottom.

His disappointment at being discarded by England was compensated somewhat by being elected Bristol captain for the 1982/83 season. It was a seminal moment for the club and a great honour for him. In a season abundant with rugby riches, the jewel was undoubtedly the 28-22 Cup Final victory over Leicester. Disappointingly, Bristol lost in the Cup Final the following season when Rafter was also captain but in the two seasons under his inspirational but demanding leadership Bristol won most of their 100 games.

Yet it was his scandalous omission from the 1977 and 1980 British Lions squads that hurt most. He was the nominated reserve for both tours but that was little consolation, particularly in 1980 when the only true open-side flank forward on the tour had to fly home after the first match. The replacement, a number eight, flew out and the Springboks revelled in their freedom. Instead, Rafter went on the Public School Wanderers tour of Zimbabwe which was arranged to coincide with the Lions tour.

Rafter had an outstanding game for the England and Wales XV that beat Scotland and Ireland in front of the Queen in Cardiff in 1980.

He also played for the President's XV against Wales in 1984 to celebrate the completion of the National Stadium.

He was Gloucestershire captain for seven seasons and led the side that won the County Championship in 1983 and 1984. Rafter also played for the Barbarians on 4 occasions, kicking a conversion in their match with Swansea in 1978.

Rafter relinquished the club captaincy to Polledri at the end of the 1983/84 season. He pulled a hamstring against Bath in October 1984 and although he recovered, he took the rest of the season off. By the time the next season arrived he had realised there was more to life than playing rugby and decided not to play again.

Rafter qualified as a coach whilst still playing. He coached the successful 1985 England Colts side to Canada, and also Bristol. He also guided the South West Division to their victory over Australia in 1988 and later coached Bedford, St Mary's Old Boys, Stroud, and the Gloucestershire side which won the 2002 County title.

An inspirational leader and successful businessman, Mike Rafter, or 'Rafter the Grafter' as he was affectionately known, is now a non-executive director of Bristol Rugby Club.

Bill Redwood
Scrum-half

Born: 6 February 1939

Career: 1958-69

Appearances: 243 games

Representative Honours: Gloucestershire, Western Counties, England

Tries: 56

Conversions: 47

Penalties: 19

Drop Goals: 38

Points: 433

Bill Redwood was one of Bristol's greatest scrum-halves. An innovative, inspirational match winner, he was desperately unlucky to gain only two England caps, and these came comparatively late in his career. After appearing in five England trials he finally gained his just reward when he played against Wales at Twickenham in 1968, scoring a try following a brilliant darting run in a game which ended in a 11-11 draw. He retained his place for the following game against Ireland, again at Twickenham, but was concussed after half an hour and had to leave the field. No replacements were permitted in those days and England had to withdraw a forward from the pack. This game also ended in a draw, but sadly there were to be no further caps for Redwood.

Bristol rugby was very much in Bill Redwood's blood. His father, Percy, played at scrum-half for the club before the war, and his younger brother, Bob, also played a few games, although he was chiefly associated with Cheltenham and Gloucester. Bill Redwood attended Bristol Grammar School and appeared for Bristol Public and Grammar Schools in 1955/56. He continued his education at Exeter University and was also at Worcester College, Oxford for a year, although he failed to gain a Blue while he was in residence. He actually played for Bristol United as a sixteen year old, but was considered too young to be properly playing and was listed as Brian Williams to conceal his identity – his Christian names are Brian William.

Redwood made his full Bristol debut in 1958 and he soon established a successful half-back partnership with his captain, John Blake. He won his first-team cap at the end of the 1958/59 season and played forty games the following year, winning his blazer and making the first of his nine appearances for Gloucestershire. These were vintage seasons for Bristol, and Redwood relished the speed and excitement of Bristol's revolutionary open style. He played in his first two England trials in 1960/61, appearing for the Possibles at Coventry and then for England, in the absence of the first choice scrum-half Dickie Jeeps, in the final trial at Twickenham. During this season he also partnered Blake in the Western Counties side which faced the touring South Africans at Gloucester and although the home side was swamped 42-0, Redwood himself impressed in adversity.

A combination of injuries and study curtailed Redwood's rugby over the next few seasons. He had to have a cartilage operation following a knee injury and he later fractured an arm. Bristol's supporters had to wait until 1965/66 to see him in regular action for the club again. He was close to England honours in 1966/67 when he appeared in two further trials, turning out at Brighton for the Whites and then at Twickenham for the Probables. He was also Bristol's vice-captain in this season.

Bill Redwood became Bristol's captain in 1967/68, finally gaining his long overdue international recognition after playing in the Rest team which beat England 21-5. His half-back partner in this match was club colleague Tony Nicholls. Redwood appeared in 37 matches during his first season of captaincy, dropping a remarkable 17 goals. He was not so fortunate in 1968/69 when injury struck again and he was only able to lead Bristol on ten occasions. One of these ten matches did, however, provide perfect evidence of his genius as a match winner. In November, Bristol travelled to Twickenham to meet hitherto undefeated Harlequins. That they came away with a 19-16 victory was due

almost entirely to a fantastic final half hour from Redwood during which he scored a try and dropped two goals, the second at the very end of the game.

This season saw the end of Bill Redwood's Bristol career, a career blighted by injuries, but nonetheless outstanding. It was not, however, the end of his association with the Bristol club. He took on the demanding role of fixture secretary during the 1980s, holding this office for over ten years, and was later vice-chairman and then chairman. Bristol recognised his worth by appointing him an honorary vice-president.

It seems strange that such an exciting player as Redwood was never honoured by selection for the Barbarians. As a form of consolation he did play for and captain another invitation side with a commitment to running rugby, the Penguins, with whom he toured to Zambia. Notwithstanding his comparative lack of representative recognition, he was a truly great player, capable of filling in at outside half or full-back if required. Finally, it must be recorded that Redwood's greatness was achieved despite the fact that he had only one effective eye.

Mark Regan
Hooker

Born: 26 January 1972

Career: 1991-97

Appearances: 120 games

Representative Honours: Gloucestershire Schools, England Schools 16 Group, 18 Group, England Colts, England Students, England U21, South West Division, World XV, Emerging England, England A, England, British Isles

Tries: 10

Points: 49

Mark Regan was always going to be a top rugby player. Coming from a rugby-loving family, he has played the sport all his life. From Keynsham minis he progressed through junior rugby and played for Bristol Schools, eventually becoming a British Lion.

Educated at St Brendan's College, Regan developed into a strong, physical hooker. He complemented his power with athleticism and possessed deceptive pace. He was capped by England Schools at 16 and 18 Group levels and was an accomplished swimmer, representing the South West.

A Bristol Colt from 1988 to 1991, he represented Gloucestershire Schools and played for England Colts. He progressed from the Colts to the Bristol squad and made his club debut against Rugby in September 1991. He shared the hooking berth with David Palmer and Andy Lathrope before becoming the club's first choice hooker when Palmer retired.

He was part of a robust Bristol pack which was difficult to play against. A youngster in a pack of considerable experience, Regan quickly picked up the skills required to survive in top-flight rugby. A technically superior striker, he was a good scrummager and was at his best in tight play. He practised hard on throwing into the line-out and worked well with Andy Blackmore. He was also a good support player and tackler. An engineer in the family crane business, his job helped develop his strength and fitness levels.

Regan played for England Students, England Under-21 and Emerging England before touring Australia and Fiji with England A in 1995. He scored a try for England A against France that year before representing England A against Natal in a pre-world cup friendly in Durban. He made his international debut in the first England match played in the professional era, against South Africa in November 1995. Regan played for England throughout the following two Five Nations tournaments, played in the last international played at Cardiff Arms Park, and won 13 caps in all as a Bristol player.

In 1997 Regan toured South Africa with the British Lions. He competed with future Bristol hooker Barry Williams and Keith Wood for test selection and played in the third international. He left Bristol and joined Bath on his return. His last appearance for Bristol was against Bedford in the end of season play-off at the Memorial Ground.

Regan played for Bath for 5 seasons during which he continued to play for England. A European cup-winner in 1998, Mark Regan currently plays for Leeds Tykes and is training to be a rugby coach.

Dave Rollitt

Number 8/wing forward

Born: 24 March 1943

Career: 1963-77

Appearances: 415 games

Representative Honours: Gloucestershire, Middlesex, Barbarians, Western Counties, England

Tries: 102

Points: 344

Dave Rollitt was one of the most significant and influential players to have played for Bristol. He adopted a professional approach to rugby during the amateur days and helped revolutionise the play of the number eight forward.

Educated at Barnsley Holgate Grammar School, he played rugby for Barnsley and Wakefield whilst still at school. He read physics at Bristol University and then studied at Loughborough Colleges before becoming a mathematics teacher at Colston's School.

Greatly influenced by rugby league as a youngster, Rollitt played rugby union for Bristol University and was in the side that won the UAU championship in the early 1960s. He made such an impact that he represented Western Counties against New Zealand in 1963, and played for Gloucestershire whilst a student. However, he needed to play more senior rugby so he joined Bristol, making his debut against Metropolitan Police in March 1964.

Supremely fit, he was a fanatical trainer and applied a scientific approach to his match preparations. Whilst at Loughborough he played for the college team that were runners up in the 1965 Middlesex Sevens, yet it was in the fifteen-man game that Rollitt made his name. A powerful tackler, he had remarkable anticipation of opponents' moves and his defensive positioning was outstanding. However, it was as an attacking player that Rollitt really excelled. Quick and forthright, Rollitt played in the face of his opponents. He

was one of a handful of visionary players to introduce the pick up and drive move, characteristic of number eight forwards today. The move originated in South Africa, but Rollitt helped develop it to suit British rugby.

Supremely focused on winning, he was a regular scorer and many of his 102 tries for Bristol were completed with an extravagant dive. Rollitt set records for tries scored in a season by a forward when he crossed for 20 in the 1965/66 season. He also held the record for career tries by a forward. Both these records were overtaken by Nigel Pomphrey.

Undoubtedly one of Rollitt's most important roles was that of captain. He possessed extraordinary leadership skills. Bristol appointed him captain for the 1969/70 and 1970/71 seasons and the energetic Rollitt was instrumental in appointing Peter Colston as the club's first official coach. He was captain for the 1969 Armistice Day débâcle against ASM Clermont-Ferrand when constant violence and biased refereeing forced him to threaten to take the team off the pitch, and he played in the 1973 RFU Cup final.

A distinctive figure with prematurely grey hair, he moulded his pack into a physically hard bunch capable of playing winning rugby in Wales. His strenuous efforts to make Bristol England's leading club made him a particularly popular player.

Rollitt played in England trials throughout his career but his talents were not fully appreciated until he won his first England cap in Dublin in 1967. Rollitt was then offered an attractive package to join Warrington Rugby

Bristol captain Rollitt with Andy Hoon (left) and Mike Collins (centre) prior to the last game of the 1970/71 season.

League club. Fortunately he declined, and went on tour with England to Canada before, mysteriously, being dropped.

The Press called for his recall and Rollitt played magnificently in the 1968 trials. He could not be ignored and was recalled to the side in 1969. He was at his imperious best against France and scored a try in a resounding 22-8 victory. But, again, he was dropped when playing at the top of his form.

Frustrations at the selectorial inconsistencies which saw him captain trial teams without playing for his country were compounded when he was unable to tour South Africa with England in 1972. Colston's School refused to release him though it later transpired he had been considered as tour captain.

His next appearance for England was in 1975 against Scotland, before later touring Australia with England. He played in both test matches and was approached by Western Suburbs to remain in Australia and play for them until the end of their season. He declined, but he had played his last game for England and amassed the scandalously small total of 11 caps. He had, however, set an unusual record in being selected to start internationals in all three back-row positions for England.

Rollitt played for Gloucestershire on 73 occasions, touring southern Africa with the county in 1976. He also played for the Barbarians in 16 matches and appeared regularly against touring sides, captaining Western Counties against South Africa in 1969 and Fiji in 1970. In 1971 he captained the South & South West against the President's XV as part of the RFU's centenary celebrations.

In 1977 he left Bristol to take up an appointment at St Paul's School in London. His last home game was against Gloucester in April 1977, but he pulled off the Bristol jersey for the final time after playing Selection Bassin on a French tour the following month. He joined Richmond and played for them for two seasons, and also appeared for Middlesex.

Rollitt then pursued a coaching career that saw him help develop rugby players at Aspen Colorado, Harlequins, Surrey and the South East Division before becoming director of coaching for Imperial Medicals. His son Eben played for Bristol in the 1990s and his daughter Pippa is the club physiotherapist for Rosslyn Park.

Dave Rollitt remains involved in rugby with the medical students and the youngsters at St Paul's. They are privileged, for he is one of Bristol's greatest-ever players.

Born: 7 October 1968

Career: 1987-2000

Appearances: 171 games

Representative Honours: England Schools, England B, Scotland U19, Scotland U21, Scotland

Tries: 11

Points: 51

Alan Sharp was the cornerstone of the Bristol scrum for several seasons. A formidable scrummager, he helped hold an inexperienced pack together when Bristol were in the Second Division and played an important role in securing promotion.

Educated at St Brendan's College, Sharp was influenced by rugby coach, Elwyn Price. Price guided the powerfully built youngster, who occasionally played in second and back rows, to become an England Schools international prop at Under-16 level and Avon Schools shot-put and discus champion. Sharp was later capped at Under-18 level and captained the Bristol Colts team. He worked extensively on his strength and was once advised to stop weightlifting in case he became muscle-bound.

He made his debut for St Brendan's Old Boys at the tender age of fifteen and played once for Bristol United in the 1986/87 season. The following season he made his Bristol debut, against Weston in December, and played for Scotland Under-19, qualifying through a grandmother born in Brechin. Sharp was an abrasive player who never took a backward step. Squat and stocky, he tormented taller props whom he was able to

manoeuvre underneath, and had the technique to make life uncomfortable for all his opponents.

He played for England B in 1989, but kept his international options open by representing the Anglo Scots and Scottish Exiles. He played through pain in a Scotland trial in 1992/93 and was selected to make his debut against Ireland shortly afterwards. Unfortunately, on the eve of the match he was diagnosed with a fractured leg, and had to wait until Scotland played England the following season to make his debut. He won a total of 6 caps.

Appendicitis precluded him from Scotland's South Seas tour in 1993 but he toured Argentina in 1994. His career was regularly interrupted by injuries, and he missed the 1995 World Cup.

Sharp left Bristol in November 1990 and joined Clifton before returning to the Memorial Ground for the 1992/93 season. He left again, this time for Coventry, at the end of the 1995/96 season, returning once more when Bristol were battling in the Second Division. Sharp, who still lived in the city, was asked if he could alleviate an injury crisis at Bristol. He rejoined and provided essential experience in the promotion campaign.

Alan Sharp retired at the end of the 1999/2000 season due to a back injury. His last match was against Henley in the Tetley's Bitter Cup. He is now landlord of The Bear and Rugged Staff pub on Southmead Road.

Mervyn Shaw
Prop

Born: 22 March 1897

Died: 21 July 1978

Career: 1919-29

Appearances: 290 games

Representative Honours: Gloucestershire, Gloucestershire & Somerset XV

Tries: 8

Points: 24

Mervyn Shaw was one of the toughest forwards to have played for Bristol. He was described as 'a strong, fire-eating pack leader' and was the most devoted of Bristol men, serving the club as player and administrator for many years.

A timber merchant at Avonmouth docks, Shaw served as a sergeant-major in the Royal Artillery during the First World War. He was in France for three and a half years and whilst there played rugby for the 10th RGA Corps and the 2nd Army Corps.

Having first played for Avonmouth as a fifteen year old, he joined his older brother Clifford at Bristol after the war and made an impressive debut in a 21-3 home victory over Cardiff in September 1919. His prowess as a prop and his leadership skills were such that he played for Gloucestershire shortly afterwards, and appeared in the county championship winning side later that season.

Shaw formed a fearsome front row with Sam Tucker and Fred Coventry, the three playing as a unit on more than 250 occasions for Bristol. They also played regularly for Gloucestershire.

Shaw had trials for England and many considered him unfortunate not to have been capped. He captained Gloucestershire and the combined Gloucestershire and Somerset XV that played New South Wales in 1927.

He was vice-captain of Bristol in 1921/22 and 1927/28, and was elected Bristol captain for the 1928/29 season. It was a successful season which concluded with a tour to Devon and Cornwall.

He was nominated by his fellow players to remain captain for the following season but at the annual general meeting a counter nomination from non-playing members that Sam Tucker should be captain was received, and despite protestations, Shaw was outvoted. A man of principle, Shaw resigned from the club with his friend 'Barty' Stinchcombe, and joined Bath. His last game for Bristol was at Redruth in April 1929.

He played for Bath for several seasons, and captained the club before retiring and helping out at Horfield Church RFC, playing occasionally for Elders & Fyffes at Avonmouth. He patched up his differences with Bristol and served on the committee after the Second World War. He chaired ground and selection committees but resigned at the end of the 1952/53 season when his son, Ray, became a United player, to avoid accusations of nepotism.

The most fanatical of rugby men, Mervyn Shaw helped coach Bristol and various Combination clubs into the 1960s, and supported Bristol until his death in 1978.

Born: 1 May 1950

Career: 1974-89

Appearances: 432 games

Representative Honours: Gloucestershire, South West, England, Barbarians

Tries: 7

Points: 28

Austin Sheppard, a long-serving tight head prop for Bristol, won 2 England caps. The first of these was in 1981, when he replaced hamstring victim Fran Cotton in the first half of the 21-19 defeat against Wales in Cardiff. England captain Bill Beaumont moved Gloucester prop Phil Blakeway to Cotton's loose head position, allowing Sheppard, who was so unfamiliar to the England chairman of selectors that he mistook Sheppard for Gloucester's Gordon Sargent, to play in his specialist front-row place. Despite England's defeat the pack played well together and there was much local delight that the popular Sheppard had been capped on what was his first call-up to the England squad. Sadly, he was not even amongst the replacements for England's next game and he had to wait until 1985 for his second cap, as a loose-head, when he appeared in the final match of the championship, again at Cardiff, when Wales won 24-15. He also toured New Zealand with England at the end of the season, playing in the undefeated midweek team.

Sheppard attended Colston's School where he captained the First XV with Alan Morley as his vice-captain. During his schooldays he appeared for Bristol Public and Grammar Schools and Somerset Schools, and also had an England hockey trial. An apprenticeship in funeral directing took him to London, where he joined Harlequins, playing for their lower sides as a number 8 forward. On returning to Bristol he became a member of Old Colstonians, captaining them for two seasons and appearing in over 100 consecutive games. He made his Bristol debut as a second row at Pontypool in 1974, but was switched to prop at the end of the season. The following season he made 37 appearances and won his Bristol cap. He played 43 matches in 1975/76, won his blazer in 1977 and led the forward appearances with 40 in 1977/78.

Austin Sheppard made 26 appearances for Gloucestershire, including the finals of 1977, 1981 and 1983. He went on the 1985 Barbarians Easter tour and also played in various local selections against tourists, facing Australia and New Zealand twice each and Romania once. He continued to be a Bristol regular into the 1980s, frequently partnering Kevin Bogira and John Doubleday in the front row. They played together in 1983 when Bristol won the cup and Sheppard also played in the 1984 final. He was Bristol's vice-captain in 1981/82 and played his greatest number of games in a season in 1983/84, when he appeared 46 times. His last full season was 1985/86, after which he played only occasionally, choosing to devote more time to coaching.

Harry Sherman
Wing

Born: Unknown

Died: Unknown

Career: 1925-36

Appearances: 224 games

Representative Honours: Somerset, Gloucestershire & Somerset XV

Tries: 170

Drop Goals: 3

Points: 522

Harry Sherman, a winger who learnt his rugby at Colston's School, was leading try-scorer for Bristol's second team, then known as the A XV, in 1925/26, touching down 24 times. Injuries to Reg Pickles and Tom Spoors resulted in him getting a few first-team games and he was soon impressing with his speed and clever finishing. From 1926, when he became a regular in the team, until 1935, when business frequently took him away from rugby, he established a reputation as something of a try-scoring machine, regularly ending the season as Bristol's leading scorer.

Sherman first topped the try-scoring list in 1926/27 with 18 and his best effort came two years later when he scored 26. 21 tries in 1931/32 and 17 the following season were again enough to top the list, as were his 17 in 1934/35, by which time he was enjoying the service of Ronnie Morris in the centre. He captained Bristol in 1933/34, but was unfortunate to be out of the side for a long period with injury. Even so, he scored 12 tries in just 18 appearances.

Sherman, who was also a promising cricketer, played county rugby for Somerset, appearing in the County Final defeat against Lancashire at Bath in 1935. He also played for the combined Gloucestershire and Somerset side which lost 23-3 to the 1935 All Blacks at Bristol. He scored one of Bristol's tries in the sensational 28-14 victory at Cardiff in 1930, Bristol's last win there until 1972. Two seasons after the 1930 triumph, Cardiff visited Bristol with a star-studded side containing the potential Welsh three-quarter line. The Bristol team had won its previous 14 games and the match was billed as a mini-international. A close, exciting game finished in a 5-0 win for Bristol, with Sherman scoring the only try.

Harry Sherman's final career record makes impressive reading. He was not forgotten by the club after he retired and was invited to attend a special reunion for past captains during Bristol's centenary year. He and Bill Woodward were the only pre-war skippers present at this historic gathering.

Harry Shewring
Centre

Born: 26 April 1882

Died: 27 November 1960

Career: 1901-13

Appearances: 251 games

Representative Honours: Somerset, England

Tries: 67

Conversions: 43

Penalties: 17

Drop Goals: 17

Points: 406

Harry Shewring was one of the best centre three-quarters in England during the early years of the twentieth century. He gained 10 England caps, making him, after W.R. Johnston, the most capped Bristol player of the pre-First World War era. He made his England debut against Ireland in 1905, only missed 2 of the next 11 internationals, and in 1907 he was the only English three-quarter to keep his place for the entire season. He featured in several historic matches, including England's first games against New Zealand, South Africa and France. England first played France in Paris in 1906, and although Shewring did not score on this occasion, he scored 1 of his country's 9 tries in the return fixture at Richmond a year later. This was his only international try.

Shewring attended Colston's School in Bristol and played his early club rugby for the original Keynsham club. He made his Bristol debut on 2 March 1901 as a full-back against Rosslyn Park, but as the decade progressed he became firmly established at centre, although he made occasional appearances at outside half. He was appointed captain for the 1907/08 season, a moderate season for the club in which only 18 games were won, although the second half of the season was considerably better than the first. Shewring was also captain of Somerset during this season and in total played 43 games for the county.

Harry Shewring played no fewer than 3 times against the original All Blacks, appearing for both Bristol and Somerset against the tourists in addition to featuring in the England game. Outside internationals, his only other game against a touring side came surprisingly late in his career when he appeared in the Somerset side which lost 24-3 to the Second Springboks at Bath in 1912. In 1910 he was invited along with club colleagues Maurice Neale and Jack Spoors to join the British team to tour South Africa but, to use the quaint language of Bristol's annual report for that season, he 'declined the invitation.' It is a shame that the South African public was denied the opportunity of seeing this gifted player in action.

David Sorrell

Outside half/centre/full-back

Born: 17 September 1956

Career: 1973-93

Appearances: 369

Representative Honours: Gloucestershire, South & South West, England U23, England B

Tries: 49

Conversions: 297

Penalties: 274

Drop Goals: 29

Points: 1,699

David Sorrell was one of the most prolific point-scorers in Bristol's history. A versatile back, equally happy at outside half, centre or full-back, he enjoyed a lengthy spell with Bristol and received many representative honours.

Sorrell was rugby captain at Henbury School for four years and played for Bishopston first team when he was sixteen. He joined Bristol Colts and captained Gloucestershire at this level before making his first-team debut at outside half at Leicester in 1973. He gained his first team cap the following season and in 1975/76 played 41 games, scoring 203 points. In 1976/77 he played for Gloucestershire as full-back and centre and was selected for the first overseas tour by an England Under-23 team. This side visited Canada, and played two 'tests' against the full Canadian team, winning both. Sorrell was full-back for both matches, kicking goals on each occasion.

Sorrell continued with England Under 23 over the next two seasons. He appeared in three County finals for Gloucestershire at outside half, losing to Lancashire in 1980 and Northumberland in 1981 before tasting victory against Yorkshire in 1983. He continued to flourish at Bristol, scoring 201 points in 1978/79 and playing a significant part in the club's run of 17 victories at the end of the season. His kicking during this period was well nigh faultless and he was unfortunate to be injured early in 1979/80 when he looked set to continue his rich vein of form. Even so, he managed 178 points in this season.

Sorrell's points-scoring reached new heights in 1981/82 when he amassed 321 and played a major role in another winning run, this time of 14 games. Having previously been a replacement at England trials, he played for the South and South West in 1980/81 and was awarded his England B cap in December 1982 when he played at outside half and kicked a penalty in a 10-6 victory over Ireland in Belfast. Shortly after this came his County Final glory, but an injury in Bristol's cup quarter-final at West Hartlepool, coupled with the arrival of Stuart Barnes, meant that he was only a replacement in the 1983 Cup Final.

Sorrell's first-team appearances dwindled as the 1980s progressed. His final first-team game came long after his supposed retirement when, in February 1992, he solved an injury crisis by playing at Exeter. As was so often the case, David Sorrell did not let Bristol down, kicking three penalties in a 17-12 victory.

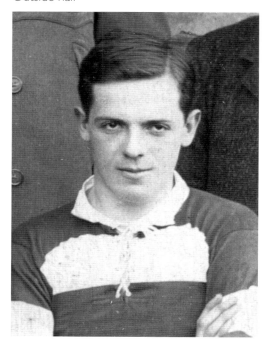

Born: c. 1884

Died: 19 March 1963

Career: 1904-11

Appearances: 182 games

Representative Honours: Gloucestershire, England trialist, British Isles

Tries: 94

Conversions: 2

Points: 286

John 'Jack' Spoors was the catalyst of Bristol's attacking play during the early years of the twentieth century. He also retains a curious international rugby record although he was never capped by his country.

Spoors was educated at Colston's School. He joined Bristol in 1903/04 and played for the Second XV before making his first-team debut against Cardiff the following season.

He had a deceptive turn of pace and possessed that rare ability to swerve and sidestep whilst running at top speed. Spoors's ball handling was of the highest order. He honed his handling skills playing cricket for Bristol Bohemians. His many talents made him one of the most elusive runners in England and a favourite with supporters.

Yet he never played rugby for England. He was a regular for Gloucestershire and he played for Bristol against New Zealand in 1905, a game in which he impressed the visitors despite a heavy defeat.

Spoors played in all three England trials during the 1909/10 season. Selected at centre for the first match, he scored a try in the Rest

XV which beat England. He was promoted to the England side which defeated the North at Birkenhead, scoring 2 tries. However, the selectors chose the Harlequins backs en bloc for the match against Wales, the first international at Twickenham, and Spoors missed out.

His silky skills had not gone unnoticed, and he was invited to tour with the 1910 British Isles team in South Africa. Spoors was the 'midfield wizard' who gave the tourists backs their cutting edge. He played in all 3 internationals and scored a try in each. That is a record which remains today. No player has ever scored a try in each international in a test series for the British Isles.

He was a prolific try-scorer at home too. He was Bristol's leading try scorer in the 1905/06 and 1908/09 seasons. During 1909/10 he moved from outside half to centre and finished top try-scorer again. He also played in the Gloucestershire side that won the County Championship for the first time. Spoors was Bristol vice-captain for the 1908/09 season, and club captain for 1910/11. At the end of that season he retired from playing, his last match being against Leicester in April 1911.

Jack Spoors continued to serve the club on the committee. He was one of five Spoors brothers to play for Bristol. The youngest, Tom, was a winger in the side throughout the 1920s.

Peter Stiff

Lock

Born: 1 April 1958

Career: 1978-95

Appearances: 360 games

Representative Honours: Somerset, England U23, South West Division, England B

Tries: 84

Conversions: 18

Penalties: 4

Points: 386

Peter Stiff was a powerful forward who provided Bristol with reliability, consistency and presence in tight play. He was also very mobile and a great favourite with Bristol supporters.

Educated at Hartcliffe Comprehensive, Stiff was initially a goalkeeper, particularly adept at dealing with the ball in the air. He used these ball-handling skills later when he played rugby, at first for Bristol Harlequins, whose captain was future referee Ed Morrison. He also played for Somerset Colts and joined Bristol Colts in 1975.

Stiff made his Bristol United debut against Old Hamptonians in 1976/77 in a side which included John Pullin. He played Colts and occasional United rugby for two seasons before making his full debut against Gloucester in September 1978.

In the early 1980s, Stiff formed a powerful partnership with Nigel Pomphrey. They were both exponents of the tapped penalty and Stiff was virtually unstoppable from ten metres. He provided a valuable nuisance factor in the line-out and was a great scrummaging lock. He also played for England Under-23 and was an occasional goal kicker.

He scored 15 tries during the 1980/81 season and was voted Supporters' Player of the Year, an award he received again ten years later. Alan Morley is the only other player to have received this award twice. Originally appointed captain of Bristol United for

1990/91, Stiff made 35 first-team appearances. He also played for the South & South West against Australia in 1981.

After Stiff played in a club game at Newbridge, England selector Derek Morgan suggested he should consider becoming a prop. He played as a tight head for a while and represented England B in this position, but he didn't enjoy it and returned to the second row.

Stiff played in the semi-final of the cup in 1983. Although he missed the 1983 final, he played in the final the following year. A regular Somerset player, he also played in the 1984 County final against Gloucestershire. He was the only player to appear for the losing side in both 1984 finals.

He considered retiring after Bristol's 1993 tour to Canada, but injuries in the club meant the loyal Stiff continued to play until a knee injury forced his retirement. His last game was against the Army in November 1994. He served on the committee and managed Bristol's tour to America in 1995.

In addition to making 360 appearances for Bristol, Stiff also played 197 games for Bristol United, scoring 65 tries. Peter Stiff was one of the greatest servants of the Bristol club.

Mark Tainton
Outside half

Born: 10 March 1965

Career: 1984-97

Appearances: 240 games

Representative Honours: England Colts, South West Division

Tries: 19

Conversions: 416

Penalties: 366

Drop Goals: 17

Points: 2,063

Mark Tainton is the most prolific points-scorer in the history of the Bristol club, and is now one of the leading authorities on goal kicking in the world.

Although from a predominantly soccer family, he was introduced to rugby at Chase School for Boys where he played as a centre. He played rugby for Cleve junior teams where he came under the influence of Arthur Sheppard. The former Bristol lock forward, who had played under John Blake, had a great influence and provided considerable encouragement.

Tainton progressed to Bristol Colts, where he was coached by Elwyn Price. He was moved to outside half where his small build and superb kicking skills were better suited. Tainton played for Bristol Colts from 1981 to 1984, captaining the team. He also played for and captained England Colts.

He made his United debut against Newport when a seventeen year old and appeared for them on several occasions whilst still a Colt. He made his full debut in the unlikely setting of Hanover in September 1984 on the club's visit to Bristol's twin city.

Tainton was a good striker of the ball. His timing when kicking from hand was immaculate and he was able to kick substantial distances,

rarely missing touch. His place kicking was accurate and his range considerable. As a runner, he had good acceleration and was quick over short distances.

He played regularly for thirteen seasons and in 1993/94 he scored 304 points for Bristol. He holds career records for conversions kicked (416) and penalties scored (366), and holds the club's overall points record of 2,063. He kicked 7 penalty goals against Leicester in 1994 and twice converted eleven tries in a match. He scored 196 points during the 1994/95 league campaign, a total only surpassed by Felipe Contepomi in 2001/02.

Tainton's last game for Bristol was at home to West Hartlepool at the end of the 1996/97 season. He then accompanied England on their summer tour to Argentina as kicking coach.

Tainton, who previously worked as an electrical engineer, has been in demand as a kicking coach ever since he stopped playing. He coached Richmond for two seasons and was involved in Oxford University's preparations for the 1999, 2000 and 2001 Varsity matches. He has advised the Australian Rugby Union on kicking techniques and helped the Irish national squad when coached by Brian Ashton.

Currently working with England Under 21s, A and elite squad members, Mark Tainton is a technical advisor and skills coach to the Bristol first-team squad.

Tommy Thompson

Forward

Born: 12 March 1868

Died: 18 December 1899

Representative Honours: Gloucestershire, Transvaal

Club records of appearances or scores were not kept at this time

In March 1939, Bristol's Old Players' Society held a dinner to commemorate its tenth anniversary. Included on the cover of the menu was a photograph of 'The late W (Tommy) Thomson to whom we owe so much'. Thomson had died in 1899 and it is significant that forty years later his contribution to the Bristol club was still remembered.

Without Thomson it is unlikely that the club would have survived. Bristol's second season, 1889/90, was a disaster. Only three matches were won and eight tries scored. Two appointed captains left, and the team often took the field short of players. Such a situation required a gifted leader and such a man was Thomson. He was appointed captain for the following season and within two years had transformed the club. The 1891/92 record showed 20 wins out of 24 games. He captained Bristol for four seasons, missing only one game when he was playing for Gloucestershire.

Tommy Thomson was a charismatic figure. He devoted himself completely to Bristol, training regularly and instilling discipline in his players. He was quiet, well-built, kind, genial, well-read and, as a good handler of men, had the respect of his team-mates.

Thomson, a former player with the Carlton club, was a founder member of Bristol. He was usually a forward although he sometimes played at centre. He also boxed and was a member of Redcliff Rowing Club.

Thomson became one of Bristol's first life members in 1894. By then he was held in such esteem that the club tried to run a testimonial fund for him, much to the annoyance of the English Rugby Union. Business took him to South Africa at the end of his fourth season of captaincy and he captained Transvaal in 1895.

Bristol welcomed him back in 1896 as vice captain and committee member but he died three years later following a bout of influenza which developed into pneumonia. Bristol's minute book of the time includes two press reports of his funeral service at St Nicholas' Church, and the club met all the funeral expenses and paid for his headstone in Arnos Vale Cemetery. The annual report of 1900 reproduces a poem by one Arthur Charlton Rigby which includes the lines:

'Goodbye Old Tommy, the heart will swell and tears unbidden rise;
But surely the sob of a sorrow'd friend the world will not despise.'

His memorial stands today in the shape of the club he rescued and restored back in the 1890s.

John Thorne

Hooker

Born: 1 January 1934

Career: 1955-71

Appearances: 287 games

Representative Honours: Gloucestershire, Territorial Army, South & South West, Western Clubs, Western Counties, England

Tries: 12

Points: 36

John Thorne was Bristol's hooker for many years. A proud Bristolian, he was a devout rugby enthusiast and played for England.

He began playing rugby at Speedwell Secondary School before representing Bristol Schools and joining Cleve RFC. Originally a back-row player, he moved up to the front row where his hooking skills were soon recognised. He captained junior and senior Combination teams and played once for Bristol United, as a flank forward, during the 1951/52 season.

Thorne served as a military policeman on National Service in Austria before returning to Cleve. He joined Bristol for the 1955/56 season, succeeding Don Woodward as hooker, and made his debut against Clifton that September. He was ideally suited to the fifteen-man style of rugby Bristol played at the time. A mobile and extremely powerful hooker, he was particularly prominent in open play.

His talents were noted by the perceptive J.V. Smith who wrote the following in programme pen pictures during the 1958/59 County Championship: Thorne 'charges around like a rhino in the loose; strikes like an adder in the tight.'

These qualities were also spotted by the England selectors, who chose Thorne for several international trials in the 1950s. He was selected for the three trials played during the harsh winter of 1962/63 and after the final trial at Torquay, one of the few places in Britain where rugby could be played, he was chosen to play for England against Wales a few weeks later.

Thorne's debut saw England win in Cardiff. It was not considered a significant event at the time, but it was to be a further 28 years before that feat was repeated. He played during the 1963 Five Nations Championship and then toured New Zealand and Australia on England's first overseas tour. In all, Thorne won three caps for England.

He represented Western Clubs against Canada in 1962 and Western Counties against New Zealand in 1963 and played 36 times for Gloucestershire, including the 1959 Championship final.

Bristol's vice captain for 1964/65, Thorne left the club at the end of the season and returned to Cleve. John Pullin was becoming Bristol's first-choice hooker, although Thorne regularly helped out as a prop.

He captained Cleve and was still playing for them when asked to help Bristol when Pullin was touring with the 1971 British Lions. He played eleven games at this time, his final appearance being at Newport in December 1971. The helpful Thorne also played for Newport on one occasion.

John Thorne subsequently acted as a public address announcer at the Memorial Ground for many years.

Frank Tucker
Hooker

Born: 13 September 1909

Died: 11 November 1969

Career: 1929-39

Appearances: 294 games

Representative Honours: Gloucestershire, Gloucestershire & Somerset XV

Tries: 13

Conversions: 3

Points: 45

Frank Tucker, a cousin of the great Sam Tucker, was Bristol's captain during the Jubilee season of 1937/38. Like the rest of the Tucker clan he attended St Nicholas with St Leonard's School and played for his school's Old Boys XV before joining Bristol, for whom he made his debut in December 1929, scoring a try against Old Merchant Taylors in a 16-3 victory. He played in the front row throughout his time at Bristol, but was only assured of his favoured position of hooker from 1934, after the departure of Gordon Gregory.

Tucker, whose brother Alf played 116 games for the club in the 1920s, was noted for his speed in open play and was joint leading appearance maker in 1930/31 with 35 games. He was awarded his Bristol cap at the end of the season and was again joint leader of the appearances in the next season. A year later he made his Gloucestershire debut and played for the county in most of his subsequent seasons. He was on the losing side against East Midlands in the 1934 County final at Northampton, but was a winner against the same opposition three years later when the

championship was won at Bristol. In 1935, he made his sole appearance against a touring side when he played for the Gloucestershire and Somerset XV against New Zealand at Bristol. The combined side lost 23-3 but Tucker had the satisfaction of setting up his team's only score following a clever bout of dribbling.

Frank Tucker was ill for part of the 1936/37 season and his place in the first team was taken by Norman Long, but he did not miss a game in the following season, his first as Bristol captain. This was the club's Jubilee year and Tucker's ever-present run was 39 matches of which 25 finished in victory. He was commended in the club's annual report for establishing a great team spirit and the side he led was certainly a happy one. He was captain again in 1938/39, although this time the playing record was poor and there were more defeats than victories. This was Bristol's final season of the inter-war years. A docker, Frank Tucker was in reserved occupation during the war and served in the ARP. Unfortunately the coming of war signalled the end of this loyal player's rugby days.

Sam Tucker
Hooker

Born: 1 June 1895

Died: 4 January 1973

Career: 1919-31

Appearances: 301 games

Representative Honours: Gloucestershire, Gloucestershire & Somerset XV, Barbarians, England & Wales XV, England

Tries: 16

Points: 48

Sam Tucker, a member of a rugby dynasty which provided Bristol with Mike Rafter and Frank Tucker amongst others, was one of the club's greatest ever forwards and a hugely popular player. A hooker, he played 27 games for England and captained his club, county and country.

Tucker achieved rugby immortality in January 1930 when he made a famous last-minute flight to Cardiff to play for England against Wales. Tucker had been dropped in favour of Douglas Kendrew of Woodford, but Kendrew was moved to prop when Henry Rew of Exeter was injured in training on the day before the game. The selectors did not make a final decision about Rew until the following morning and sent out an emergency call to Tucker, despite the presence in Cardiff of Bath's Norman Matthews, the travelling reserve. By the time Tucker got the news, he had missed the last train, but managed to travel from Filton Airport in a private plane which had to land in a field as there was no landing strip. Tucker had never flown before and was shaken by the landing, but recovered himself sufficiently to run across two fields to the

nearest road where he flagged down a passing lorry. The driver took him to within sight of the ground, but even then thousands of people were outside, blocking his way. Fortunately, he spotted a policeman whom he knew and he was escorted to the gates. Having sprinted round to the changing rooms, he joined his team-mates five minutes before kick-off and contributed fully to England's 11-3 victory, returning to Bristol afterwards to attend an old boys' dinner. He later wrote of his regret that Matthews, the reserve, who was changed and ready to play, never received an England cap.

Tucker had made his England debut in less happy circumstances at Cardiff eight years previously. He was unwell at the time, England lost heavily and he was not capped again until the New Zealand match of 1925. After that he became a fixture in the side, appearing in every game until the final match of 1929, and scoring tries against Scotland in 1926 and New South Wales in 1928. He retained his place following his recall in 1930 and was appointed captain for the final two internationals of the season. He made one further appearance against Wales in 1931 and was again captain on this occasion.

Sam Tucker learned his rugby at St Nicholas with St Leonard's School and was a founder member of the school's Old Boys XV, becoming its first captain. He always retained a loyal affection for his old school and its rugby-loving headmaster, Tom Barrow. Tucker fought with the South Midlands Royal Engineers in the First World War and was injured at the Battle of the

Somme. He played in Bristol's first official game when the club was relaunched in 1919 and won his first team cap at the end of the season. An England trial followed in 1920/21 and in September 1921 he played in the opening game on the Memorial Ground, scoring a try.

Tucker, Bristol's vice captain for two seasons from 1922, was a vital member of the pack during the years of success in the mid 1920s, regularly appearing in the front row with Mervyn Shaw and Fred Coventry. He became Bristol captain in 1929, but only after an unfortunate episode which resulted in Shaw's departure from the club. Shaw had been the players' nomination for the captaincy and was overlooked in favour of Tucker, but any problems Tucker had in re-establishing team spirit seem not to have affected his own form, as 1929/30 proved a season of great personal success. He captained the Gloucestershire side which won the County Championship, enjoyed his aforementioned England recall and led the combined England and Wales team in the Rowland Hill Memorial Match against Scotland and Ireland at Twickenham. In all he played 37 times for Gloucestershire, winning four championship titles and taking part in the county's draw with the Maoris. He also appeared for Gloucestershire and Somerset against New South Wales and played twice for The Barbarians. He continued as Bristol captain in 1930/31, but retired at the end of the season, playing his final game at Torquay.

Bristol were not slow to recognise Tucker's contribution to rugby in the city, holding a special dinner in his honour in 1928. Such was the popularity of 'Our Sam' that a brand of orange bore this name, the label showing a portrait of Tucker in his Bristol kit. Needless to say, in those strictly amateur days, he received no payment for this honour. Tucker was a tireless fundraiser for local rugby, arranging an annual game between Bristol and an International XV and masterminding the successful Memorial Ground carnivals. He served on the Bristol committee, was made an honorary life member in 1946 and became president of the Old Players' Society in 1967.

David Tyler

Wing/Full Back

Born: 11 November 1946

Career: 1966-77

Appearances: 425 games

Representative Honours: Somerset, Western Counties, South & South West, England trial

Tries: 154

Conversions: 4

Penalties: 5

Drop Goals: 3

Points: 543

David Tyler enjoyed a lengthy playing career with Bristol, initially as a wing or centre and latterly as a full-back. He was a centre in the Bristol Grammar School XV and played for Bristol Public and Grammar Schools and Gloucestershire Schools before having a brief spell with Old Bristolians. He played some games for Bristol United in 1965/66 and burst onto the first-team scene the following season as a powerful winger, leading the try-scorers with 25 and winning his Bristol cap. Tyler's initial season also included the first of his 53 appearances for Somerset and a place in the Western Counties side which defeated Australia 9-0 at Bristol. His remarkable rise continued in 1967/68 when he again headed the try scorers, this time with 26, and played for the Blues against the Whites in an England trial at Twickenham.

Tyler and fellow wing Mike Collins headed the appearances list in 1968/69 and the following season he topped the list on his own. He was also a late inclusion in the Western Counties team to play South Africa, appearing at centre in a 3-3 draw on a bitterly cold day at Bristol. He continued to play regularly but as the 1970s progressed he found his opportunities limited on the wing owing to the presence of Peter Knight, Alan Morley and Ken Plummer. He moved to full-back, playing in that position for the South and South West team which beat Australia 15-14 at Bath in 1973, and captained Bristol from 1974 to 1976. During his first season in charge he played in all but three of Bristol's 54 games in what was a poor season by the club's standards. There was a great improvement in 1975/76 and Bristol played some thrilling rugby under Tyler's leadership, winning 37 games and passing a thousand points.

David Tyler retired at the end of the 1976/77 season to become secretary of the Imperial Club. He returned to coach Bristol at the end of the 1970s, and guided the side which won the cup in 1983, famously leaving the ground to 'relax' with an Alistair MacLean novel to avoid the tension of a nail-biting quarter-final at West Hartlepool.

Tyler appeared for the Bristol club in yet another role in the following decade when he was appointed as a paid administrator. He is still associated with the game, currently working for the Rugby Football Union.

Dave Watt

Lock

Born: 5 July 1938

Career: 1958-75

Appearances: 512

Representative Honours: Gloucestershire, Somerset, Western Clubs, South of England, Western Counties, Barbarians, England

Tries: 52

Conversions: 1

Points: 163

David Watt was one of the biggest players to don the Bristol jersey. A second-row forward, he played for 18 seasons and at one time held the club's career appearance record. He still holds the record number of appearances for a Bristol forward, an achievement which is unlikely to be surpassed.

Dave Watt was born in Bristol and educated at Kingsdown Secondary School and Bristol Cathedral School. He had little interest in rugby as a boy, preferring soccer, and upon leaving school played centre-half for Twyford House in the Downs League, also regularly playing water polo.

He first played rugby by chance when a friend invited him to play for Bristol YMCA against Brentry Hospital in 1956. He joined Bristol Harlequins shortly afterwards where he discovered the social side of rugby. He quickly graduated to the firsts and played there for the remainder of the season.

A rugby novice, he joined St Mary's Old Boys the following season, but was soon invited to a trial with Bristol. He played for the United for most of the 1957/58 season and in the April played twice for the First XV as a number 8, and scored a try. Watt arrived at the Memorial Ground as 'the Blake era' was developing. The open, carefree style of play suited him and under the eye of John Blake and his experienced forwards Watt blossomed into a powerful, athletic forward. He was very mobile for such a big man, and he excelled at sevens.

The son of a Welsh father, Watt was invited to attend a Welsh trial in 1961. However following advice from fellow second row John Currie, he opted for the country of his birth and played in several England trials throughout the 1960s before, eventually, making his England debut against Ireland in Dublin in 1967.

He played in all England's championship games that season and toured Canada with England during the following summer, but although he played in many subsequent trials and toured South Africa with England in 1972, he was never capped again.

Watt has since pondered whether he was right to take Currie's advice. His replacement in the Welsh trial, Keith Rowlands, went on the British Lions tour to South Africa at the end of that season, and while there was stability in second row selection in Wales during the 1960s, England tried countless players in 'the boiler house'.

The England selectors, who struggled to appreciate the change of approach Blake had influenced at Bristol, accused him of being 'too loose' to be a successful second row. Watt is now regarded as a player ahead of his time. He had the physique and reputation which instilled fear in his opponents. He never shirked a challenge and having faced the greatest players of his era,

continued

including the legendary All Black Colin Meads, he is proud to have had the better of each. His most difficult opponent was Brian Price of Newport.

Watt played for Western Clubs against Canada in 1962, and had a super game for Western Counties against Australia in 1966. The following season he took on New Zealand for South of England, then captained Western Counties against the All Blacks in 1972.

A popular figure, Watt, who was a representative for Rothmans, played for the Barbarians in eight matches, touring South Wales at Easter on three occasions. He scored a try against Cardiff in 1971.

He played for Gloucestershire on 60 occasions and captained them for the 1971/72 season. Gloucestershire then selected John Fidler in the second row and Watt was discarded. He subsequently played for Somerset in 1973/74, qualifying by residence.

Watt was Bristol's vice captain in 1971/72 and played in the 1973 Cup Final. In 1974/75 he passed 500 appearances for the club and was made an honorary vice-president. The club held

a dinner in his honour. He pulled a hamstring at Newbridge in April 1975 and although he recovered in time to tour Canada with the club at the end of the season, he suffered a further leg injury in training and was forced to retire.

He served on the committee until the 1984/85 season, playing occasional charity games. He was a replacement for the Public School Wanderers against the Cantabrians in 1979, at the Memorial Ground. When he came on for the injured Steve Boyle mid way through the second half he played once more on a pitch he had first graced over twenty years before.

He left Bristol to coach and manage Old Crescent in Ireland for three seasons after which he moved on to St Austell where he took up a similar role. He now runs his own business in Bodmin and helps out occasionally with the Bodmin club and at Wadebridge.

At the end of the 1960/61 season Watt was presented with his Bristol club blazer, having passed 70 appearances. The measure was the biggest ever for a Bristol player. But then that was Dave Watt: big heart, big man, great player.

Laurie Watts
Centre

Born: 2 May 1935

Died: 26 August 1997

Career: 1956-64

Appearances: 124 games

Representative Honours: Gloucestershire, Western Counties, England trial

Tries: 42

Conversions: 43

Penalties: 26

Drop Goals: 2

Points: 296

Laurie Watts, a centre during the Blake era, was desperately unlucky not to play for England. He appeared in trials, was a travelling reserve throughout 1958 and was on standby for England's visit to Dublin in 1959 as there was a doubt over the fitness of England captain Jeff Butterfield. Unfortunately for Watts, Butterfield decided to play, although he implied to Watts that a cap was sure to be his in future seasons. Sadly this was not to be and in November 1960 Watts broke his wrist playing against London Welsh on the day that he received news of an England trials call-up. He played no rugby until the following March, and his chance was not to come again.

Laurie Watts is probably the only Bristol player to have a street named after him, his builder father naming Laurence Grove in Dursley after his young son. An all-round sportsman, Watts captained Bristol Grammar School at cricket and rugby. At seventeen, while still at school, he played Second XI cricket for Gloucestershire and rugby for Clifton. He continued both sports at Wadham College, Oxford, gaining rugby Blues in 1957 and 1958, and narrowly missing a cricket Blue. He continued his cricket with Gloucestershire and made one first-class appearance in 1958.

Watts caused a sensation on the Oxford and Cambridge tour of the Far East in 1959, scoring 34 points against Ceylon Barbarians. This total was a world record for many years. He created great interest on this tour with his 'round the corner' style of place kicking, then very much an innovation. Watts had special boots made without toecaps and kicked with his instep.

Laurie Watts's Bristol career was interrupted by university and national service. He switched to centre from his school position of outside half while with Bristol United. He was a superb reader of a game and a great timer of a pass, always ensuring that his passes never exposed a team-mate to danger. He ran with the ball held in both hands, prepared to dummy, sidestep, accelerate or pass. He played 25 times for Gloucestershire, appearing in the 1959 County Final, and was in the Oxford University and Western Counties teams which beat the 1957 Australians.

Asthma finally brought Laurie Watts's playing career to an end. By then he had moved to Wales where he became one of the Welsh Rugby Union's top referees, later acting as an assessor. When his sons were at Monmouth School he became assistant coach there. He lived at Crickhowell for many years, where he served as a lay reader and churchwarden. A memorial bench in the churchyard commemorates this popular and talented sportsman.

Jonathan Webb
Full Back

Born: 24 August 1963

Career: 1985-90

Appearances: 122 games

Representative Honours: England Students, South West Division, England B, England

Tries: 47

Conversions: 148

Penalties: 110

Points: 814

Jonathan Webb was one of the finest attacking full-backs English rugby has seen. An accomplished goal kicker, he later held career points and appearance records for England.

A Londoner, Webb came to Bristol to study medicine at the university. Brought up in Newcastle, he ran the 400 metres for English Schools, and played rugby initially at scrum-half, then outside half. He joined Northern as a wing before switching to full-back.

Webb played for Bristol University and although he attracted interest from Bristol, he was encouraged to remain a University player until his studies were complete. He played for Bristol United towards the end of the 1984/85 season before formally joining Bristol during the summer. His debut for Bristol was the infamous match against Newport in 1985 when referee George Crawford walked off following several bouts of fighting. It was a black day for Bristol, but Webb's emergence was an enormous positive from a day of negatives.

Webb was an elegant player possessing deceptive pace and his incursions into the line were completed with perfect timing. He was also a highly proficient goal kicker and defensively sound. England couldn't ignore

him, and in his second season with Bristol he was chosen for the national squad. A bench replacement in 1987, he went to the inaugural World Cup as Marcus Rose's understudy. When Rose was injured against Australia, Webb made his debut and remained in the side for the rest of the tournament. The following year he toured Australia, and won 17 caps in all as a Bristol player. He was also a member of the South West team that defeated Australia in 1988.

During the 1989/90 season Webb struggled to maintain his previously high standards of play. His form dipped and he lost his England place. Balancing medical studies with a rugby career became difficult so he decided to give up rugby, his last game for Bristol being against Clifton in early 1990.

After a few weeks his family encouraged him to reconsider. Webb felt a return to Bristol could cause the problems to recur so he joined Bath. Although not courted by Bath, this move resurrected his career. He regained his England place, played in the 1991 World Cup and scored a record 67 points in the 1992 Five Nations Championship, including 3 tries. A Grand Slam winner that year, he was honoured as one of rugby's Five Players of the Year for 1992, and became England's most capped full-back.

Retiring in 1993, Jonathan Webb currently provides medical support to Bristol and is an orthopaedic surgeon at Southmead Hospital.

David Weeks
Centre

Born: 30 December 1935

Career: 1958-65

Appearances: 213 games

Representative Honours: Gloucestershire, Western Counties, Ghana

Tries: 50

Points: 150

David Weeks was one of a crop of talented backs who flourished under the innovative leadership of John Blake. He was usually selected as a centre but also featured in games on the wing and, occasionally, at outside half. He scored 50 tries for Bristol, his 50th coming in his 200th game.

Weeks learned his rugby at Bristol Grammar School, played for Gloucestershire Schools and then Bristol University, where he was captain of the First XV. He gained his Bristol United cap at the end of his first season at Bristol during which he played 18 first-team games. Thereafter he was more or less a fixture in the side right up until the time of his retirement from top rugby. In 1959/60 he played 36 times and scored 16 tries to finish second to Mike Ellery in the try-scoring list. He also gained his Bristol cap and made the first of his thirteen appearances for Gloucestershire. The following season was another memorable one for him as he was selected to play for Western Counties against South Africa at Gloucester. There were nine Bristol players in all in the Counties side, but they were outclassed by the Springboks, who won 42-0. During the second half of the season Weeks stood in for the injured John Blake at outside half and was awarded his club blazer at the season's close.

David Weeks became Bristol's vice captain in 1961/62 and was a member of the team which produced a superb exhibition of rugby under the Ninian Park floodlights, defeating Cardiff 20-3. At the start of the following season he had a sensational game against Roundhay at the Torquay Festival, scoring four first-half tries in Bristol's 22-3 win, where one of the opposing centres was British Lion Jeff Butterfield. Strangely, he only scored a further four during the rest of what was to prove a somewhat protracted season due to the severe winter weather.

Weeks was recalled to the Gloucestershire side in 1963 after an absence of two seasons, appearing in the 19-9 semi-final defeat against Lancashire at Bristol. He then played a further season for the county in what was to be his last year as a Bristol player. His final season saw him play in 32 Bristol games and score 9 tries. He carried on playing for Old Bristolians for a number of years until injury finally forced his retirement from the game, although at the age of 45 he gained long-desired international honours when as an ex-pat he played for Ghana against Nigeria!

John White
Hooker

Born: 16 May 1943

Career: 1967-76

Appearances: 221 games

Representative Honours: Somerset, Barbarians, England tourist

Tries: 16

Conversions: 1

Points: 64

John White, one of the finest hookers ever to play for Bristol, was unfortunate that his time at the club coincided with that of England hooker John Pullin. Despite this, he made a huge contribution to the club and when Pullin was unavailable, either through representative calls or the demands of farming, Bristol had in White a deputy of the highest quality. After one game in 1967/68, he appeared regularly from 1968 to 1976 and from 1971 to 1976 he played 159 times to Pullin's 51.

White went to St Brendan's College and played for St Mary's Old Boys, captaining then as a 21 year old, before joining Bristol. He played 23 games during 1968/9, gaining the first of his 35 Somerset caps. He appeared in 33 games in Bristol's record-breaking season of 1971/72 and he appeared opposite Pullin in an England trial in 1973. He was a bench replacement for England and was selected to go on England's short tour to New Zealand in 1973. His opportunities were limited there, but he did play in the match against Wellington, a game England lost 25-13.

The 1972/73 season also provided John White and the Bristol club with a particularly frustrating afternoon when Pullin was injured in the first minute of the 1973 Cup Final. Club replacements were not allowed at the time and White watched from the stands as Bristol lost 27-15 to Coventry.

It is interesting to compare the respective talents of John Pullin and John White. At his peak, Pullin had no rival as a quick heeler of a ball, but White was the better thrower at line-outs, a skill much appreciated by Bristol's great forward Dave Watt. White captained Somerset from 1973 to 1975, leading the county on its tour to Canada in 1974. He played for the Barbarians against Coventry in 1973 and was on standby for England's overseas tours of 1972 and 1975.

White was Bristol's vice captain in 1973/74 and was nominated for the Bristol captaincy at the end of that season. This would have caused great problems for the club as John Pullin intimated that he might have to leave Bristol if he were not guaranteed a first-team place, but a difficult situation was avoided when White, putting club interests before his own, asked for his nomination to be withdrawn. He continued with Bristol for two more seasons, finishing with a career total of 221 games. He then returned to St Mary's as player-coach, continuing to play for the first team until he was 40. He served as club chairman and was heavily involved in organising the move to St Mary's current ground.

Chris Williams
Centre

Born: 25 December 1950

Career: 1970-83

Appearances: 310 games

Representative Honours: England Schools, South & South West, Gloucestershire

Tries: 60

Points: 239

Chris Williams was one of the most powerful and resourceful of all Bristol centres. An aggressive tackler, he played in the Bristol three-quarter line for nearly 13 seasons.

A supporter of Bristol since the age of nine, he joined the club at nineteen, having been capped as a schoolboy by England. Previously an outside half with Aretians, he made his Bristol United debut as a wing at Cwmbran in April 1970, but it was as a full-back that he made his First XV debut, against Harlequins at Twickenham the following November, giving a faultless display. However, Bristol's perceptive captain, Dave Rollitt, looked carefully at Williams. He took him under his wing and helped him develop into a tough centre. He became an integral part of the team and was rarely out of the side. Williams possessed a unique tackling style which was raw, natural and ferocious. He repelled opponents' attacks with powerful 'hits' and forced countless turnovers. He never shirked a challenge, adopting the philosophy that there was no such thing as a late tackle – his opponent merely passed too early! He also had the skills to capitalise on gaps in opposition defence and made the most of any scoring opportunities that came his way. Williams was a great favourite with Bristol supporters.

He was at his best in the mid 1970s. His greatest games were in the 1973 Cup run. In the semi-final against London Welsh, Bristol turned a 15-3 half-time deficit into an 18-15 victory over a talented side. He also played courageously in the final against Coventry.

Williams's career nearly ended in 1977 when he shattered his leg in a collision at Swansea. A seven-inch plate was fitted and it is a tribute to his fitness and dedication that he came back to play rugby at all, let alone resume his career with Bristol the following season. A further fracture in 1980/81 would have forced lesser men to have called it a day, but he recovered quickly and continued playing.

He eventually retired at the end of the 1982/83 season, his last game being against Glamorgan Wanderers in January 1983. Williams also made 17 appearances for Gloucestershire, and toured with them to South Africa in 1976. In addition, he played for South and South West against Australia in 1973. Formerly a coach with Bristol United, Aretians, Frampton Cotterell, Weston and Gloucestershire, Chris Williams is now a successful businessman producing sporting and leisure wear.

Don Woodward

Hooker

Born: 28 June 1925

Died: 12 October 2002

Career: 1948-56

Appearances: 172 games

Representative Honours: Gloucestershire, England trialist

Tries: 4

Conversions: 7

Penalties: 3

Points: 35

Don Woodward, whose death was announced as this book was going to print, was Bristol's regular hooker of the early 1950s. A powerfully built player, he was the youngest of three brothers who played for the club. Bill, a back-row forward and England Schools international, played before the Second World War and captained Bristol in 1936/37, while John Woodward often played in the front row with Don and was vice captain in 1953/54. All three brothers played for Gloucestershire.

During the Second World War, Don Woodward served in the Royal Navy. He worked on HMS *Nabob*, Canada's first aircraft carrier, and survived when it was torpedoed. He later served in the south-east Pacific on a minesweeper. After the war he returned to Bristol to run his family's general store in Southville and played for the now defunct Horfield Athletic club. In 1948 he was a member of the Horfield seven which won the Bristol Combination tournament.

Woodward played occasional games for Bristol United in 1946/47 and the following season, before winning his United cap in 1948/49 when he also made a single first-team appearance. He took over the senior hooking berth when Fred Hill stepped down half-way through the 1949/50 season and fully estab-

lished himself in 1950/51 when he led the appearances with 33 games. This was the season in which he received a late call-up for the first England trial. W.B. Ferguson of Whitehaven cried off with a rib injury and Woodward replaced him in the Colours team which played against the Whites at Otley. Three Bristol forwards, Eric Hopton, Eric McCall and Dick Honeywell, were in the opposition pack and although the score was 0-0 at half time the Whites dominated the second half, winning 13-0. Unfortunately, Woodward was never selected for a trial again.

Don Woodward only played 9 first-team games in 1951/52, losing his place to Mervyn Howell, but he was first choice for the next three seasons, leading the appearances again in 1953/54 with 35 games and playing 36 matches in 1954/55. He made a further seven appearances the following season but then announced his retirement, handing on the mantle of first-team hooker to the emerging John Thorne. His final game was the 9-0 home victory against London Irish on 1 October 1955.

Don Woodward, who made one championship appearance for Gloucestershire, continued to follow rugby after his retirement, regularly attending Bristol games and keeping in close contact with fellow former players of the club.